BATTLEFIELDS OF THE CIVIL WAR

BATTLEFIELDS OF THE CIVIL WAR

A State-by-State Guide

JOHN BOWEN

CHARTWELL
BOOKS, INC.

The charge of the 14th Brigade of the Wisconsin Volunteers captured the New Orleans Battery at the Battle of Shiloh on April 7, 1862.

CONTENTS

ISBN: 0−89009−955−3

Page make-up by: Best-set Typesetter Ltd.
Typeset by: Graphicraft Typesetters Ltd.
Color separations by: Regent Publishing Services Limited
Printed by: Lee-fung Asco Printers Limited, Hong Kong.

This book was designed and produced by
FOOTNOTE PRODUCTIONS LTD.
6 Blundell Street
London N7

Editorial Director: Sheila Buff
Art Director: Ken Diamond/Art Patrol, NYC
Design Assistant: Patricia Jerina

IN MEMORY OF THE
CONFEDERATE SOLDIERS
OF LOUDOUN COUNTY VA.
ERECTED MAY 28 1908

SOUTH CAROLINA

The Beginning

Fort Sumter's command of the entrance to Charleston harbor made Union control intolerable to the new Confederate States of America. Confederate bombardment started the Civil War. This view from the harbor, the one seen by most Charlestonians that fateful morning, is also familiar to visitors today.

A strange mixture of reluctance and anticipation pervaded the languid air of Charleston, South Carolina, during the pre-dawn hours of April 12, 1861. The shoreline was ringed with deadly mortars and cannon, all pointed at the dark hulk of Fort Sumter on a manmade island at the narrow entrance to the harbor. War was imminent; citizens of both North and South exhibited a curious mixture of enthusiasm for war and a desire not to be blamed for starting it.

Great efforts to avoid armed conflict were coming to nothing. Politicians North and South had exerted enormous efforts to resolve the conflict between the two regions over slavery, economic competition and jealousy, and, especially, the divisive tariff issue — almost as abrasive as the more emotional slavery question. South Carolina had endured the affront to its sovereignty of "foreign" forces since December 20, 1860, when the state had seceded from the United States and then joined the Confederate States of America. Confederate President Jefferson Davis had sent word from Montgomery, Alabama, to exercise caution. U.S. officials likewise were hesitant to provoke the fight that was beginning to seem inevitable: When a relief ship sent in January by the outgoing President, James Buchanan, was fired upon by Confederate shore batteries, it turned back. The incoming President, Abraham Lincoln, delivered a tough Inaugural Address asserting Federal authority over the seceding states but let almost a month of inaction go by. When he decided to send a relief expedition of three ships, he advised the South Carolina governor, Francis Pickens, that the expedition would land only supplies at the fort, not reinforcements, unless it was resisted. But all this was outweighed by mistrust and strategic considerations.

Both sides had misled the other on occasion, and those three small supply ships posed a big problem for the Confederacy. Fort Sumter was brand new and formidable, with 40-foot-high brick walls 12 feet thick at the base. It mounted 60 guns but had a new garrison of only 85 men. The commander, Major Robert Anderson, had orders to remain, but he admitted to Confederate emissaries that without supplies he could not resist the powerful array of 43 guns and mortars at Forts Johnson and Moultrie (flanking the entrance to the narrow harbor), Castle Pinckney (a small island in the inner harbor off the Battery), an innovative floating battery near Moultrieville, and temporary gun emplacements at other strategic locations along the shoreline. His supplies would be exhausted by April 15, and then he would have to capitulate. The relief ships — the steamship *Baltic*, the U.S.S. *Pawnee*, and the five-gun revenue cutter *Harriet Lane* — could alter the situation.

South Carolina officials foresaw the possibility of continued Federal occupation of the fort, which commanded the entrance to one of the most important harbors in the new Confederacy; it could not be allowed to remain in unfriendly hands. By springtime, excitement had been building in Charleston for some time. State officials had been upset by Major Anderson's decision at Christmastime, 1860 to occupy the fort, believing they had an agreement with President Buchanan that Federal troops would remain at the more vulnerable forts, Moultrie and Johnson. In many minds, this change made war inevitable, and Confederate forces moved into the former Federal mainland bases and began fortifying the entire shoreline. Crowds gathered to watch the emplacement of new cannon and to look at the now beleaguered fort.

When the cannon finally opened fire at 4:30 A.M. on April 13, it was like an early Fourth of July. Civilians, aroused from their slumbers by the booming cannon, climbed to their roofs to watch the palpitating light of muzzle flashes and the explosion of shells. Spectators would be prominent through the 34 hours the fort was under siege. For men like Brigadier General P.G.T. Beauregard of Louisiana, a former West Point commandant picked by Confederate President Davis to command the attack, there was less elation than relief that the waiting was over and the final act of dissolution was occurring, mixed with the nagging uncertainty felt by all soldiers at such times.

A tragicomedy was being acted out. An ardent civilian secessionist from Virginia (which was still in the Union at that point), Edmund Ruffin, was given the honor of touching off the first shot, but he may not have done so. Fort Sumter did not immediately return the fire, but waited until after daybreak. Majoy Anderson's soldiers had a leisurely breakfast before manning their posts, and then spaced their firing to conserve ammunition. Confederate batteries opened the battle with an intense bombardment, then alternated between sporadic firing and intense flurries during the 34 hours the fort held out. Their shells damaged Fort Sumter's wall and set fire to the officers' quarters and barracks. In a day and half of firing, more

The defender of Fort Sumter, Major Robert Anderson, remains a controversial figure. Did he break an agreement to maintain the status quo by moving his troops from Fort Moultrie to Fort Sumter? A Kentuckian with Confederate sympathies, he nevertheless honored his oath as a Union officer and defended Fort Sumter as long as he could.

Edmund Ruffin, shown here in the uniform of a private, was an ardent secessionist from Virginia; he was given the honor of firing the first shot in the assault on Fort Sumter. Virginia was still in the Union at the time.

than 2,000 rounds were launched from Fort Sumter, and Confederates fired 3,500 more; but no one was killed and only eight men — four on each side — were wounded. The only fatality came as Major Anderson saluted the flag before evacuating the fort: A cartridge bag exploded, killing a crew member, Private Daniel Hough.

Fort Sumter, along with Fort Moultrie on Sullivan's Island, is now a monument operated by the National Park Service. The imposing presence of the three-story brick fort in the harbor allows the visitor to appreciate the concern of the Confederates and the quandry of Major Anderson. It looks much better today than the battered hulk that remained at war's end. Lectures

This cannonball, embedded in the wall of Fort Sumter, shows the severity of the Union bombardment during efforts to retake the fort. Although the walls were reduced to rubble, the Confederates held Fort Sumter with little loss of life until the fall of Charleston from the land side forced evacuation.

Fort Sumter bristled with cannon like this 42-pounder in a left flank casemate, but had only a small garrison when attacked. Heavily damaged during later fighting, the fort has been restored to its approximate appearance at the start of the Civil War.

and living-history demonstrations by park rangers provide some of the excitement of the period. A tour boat from the mainland deposits visitors at a dock on the left flank, and they enter through a sally port built since the Civil War.

Like other East Coast forts, Fort Sumter has accretions from later wars, when it was used by the Coast Artillery, but it still shows the wear and tear of Civil War action. Casemates — rooms in the walls of the fort — demonstrate the practice of gunnery as it existed in the mid-1860s. Along the right flank are 11 hundred-pound Parrott guns, a rifled cannon that was extremely popular throughout the Civil War. A mountain howitzer near the Right Gorge Angle, used to defend against a surprise landing by Union forces, shows how Confederates had to improvise. Several projectiles still protrude from the wall of the Left Flank, reminders of the shelling by Union batteries in 1863.

The original shape of the five-sided brick fort, one of a series authorized by Congress after the War of 1812, remains. One of its flagpoles, shot away during the Confederate bombardment, was replaced in 1928 by one of Major Anderson's descendants to honor him and his men. The museum contains a variety of relics and tells certain episodes of the fort's history in diorama and pictorial displays. A ground-level view from the esplanade along the Gorge exterior reveals how the fort dominates the entrance to the harbor.

The relatively light damage sustained by the fort in its first battle was just the beginning. As the war went on, repossession of Fort Sumter became a Union obsession, partly because the blockade was unsuccessful. There were three attacks from the sea, all ending ingloriously, even the one in April 1863 that utilized a fleet of nine ironclad vessels. Union guns threw seven million pounds of metal at the fort.

In all the bombardment, only 52 Confederate soldiers were killed. Action elsewhere on the Atlantic coast and on western rivers would find combinations of seapower and land forces winning against forts; but Fort Sumter, even though subjected to sustained Union bombardment from Morris Island after 1863, remained in Confederate hands until Charleston was taken from the rear on February 17, 1865, during Major General William T. Sherman's march to the sea and beyond. By that time, however, the fort was just a pile of broken bricks — a sign, also obsrved elsewhere during the war, that the advent of the rifled cannon had made large fixed fortifications obsolete.

Fort Moultrie has been restored to reflect its entire martial history starting with the Revolutionary War, but key features remain from its strategic role during the War Between the States. The masonry fort that exists today had received its basic shape by that time but was reinforced with sand and wood to reduce the effect of explosions. The right section of the curved forward edge holds Civil War batteries that show the alterations made by Confederates in response to technological changes in coast artillery. Along Cannon Walk, outside the walls of the fort, are a series of cannon that highlight the evolution of seacoast defense weaponry during and after the Civil War.

The site of old Fort Johnson, on the other side of the harbor, is now occupied by a research center and is not open to the public.

In a way, the historic area of Charleston was part of the siege battlefield. From the Battery, now a beautiful waterfront walkway decorated with cannon, monuments, palmettoes and flowers, people watched history taking place. The streets of the old city retain the South Carolina lowlands atmosphere, and the history of such land-

Fort Moultrie's important role in the fighting at Charleston is recalled by period cannon of the type used to assault Fort Sumter and to defend the city against later Union attacks. Displays also represent other periods in the long history of the fort.

marks as the 1844 gothic-style Huguenot Church, the 1770 Heyward-Washington House, and the 1803 Joseph Manigault mansion recall the era when General Beauregard was lionized by the ladies and gentlemen of South Carolinian society. Beauregard's statue is in Washington Square. The Citadel, old and new, stands as an example of the tradition of state military academies that exists in a number of Southern states. The academy has moved from the historic 1822 structure to a more modern college complex not far away. The graves of a number of Confederate soldiers can be found in Magnolia Cemetery.

Hunley Museum emphasizes displays on Confederate naval history, including the C.S.S. *Hunley*, the first submarine to sink a surface vessel. Named after its inventor, H.L. Hunley, who was killed in a practice dive, the submarine drove a spar torpedo into the hull of the U.S.S. *Housatonic* on February 17, 1864, and sent it to the bottom. Unfortunately, the *Hunley* itself was swamped by the wave created by the resulting explosion and went down beside its victim.

The Confederate attack on Fort Sumter was not much of a contest. Both sides were fatalistic about the outcome, and the action, in retrospect, seems more just for the look of things than contemporaries judged from news accounts at the time. The naval relief expedition, through a series of misunderstandings caused by secrecy and disagreement, waited just outside the harbor while the fort was being forced to surrender. Yet there is no mistaking the impact of the battle. The dominoes continued to fall. President Lincoln issued a call for 75,000 volunteers and militia to restore the union, an action that precipitated further acts of secession — including those of Virginia and Tennessee, which would become major battlegrounds. Baltimore citizens stoned troops being sent to protect the national capital of Washington, but Maryland remained in the union.

Except for Fort Sumter, South Carolina was removed from the main battlefields and thus escaped much of the fighting. But retribution came late in the war when General Sherman, after reaching the sea at Savannah, Georgia, turned northward. Northern feelings against South Carolina, the first state to secede, were particularly strong, and Sherman swept though like an avenging angel. No major battles were fought, but skirmishes and destruction are noted in monuments at a number of places. Beaufort (pronounced Bew-fort) Arsenal has graves of 12,000 Union soldiers and a few Confederates and the John Mark Verdier House, built about 1790, was used as a Union headquarters. Another war cemetery is at Florence. Brigadier General Barnard E. Bee, who nicknamed "Stonewall" Jackson, is buried in the cemetery of St. Paul's Episcopal Church at Pendleton, far from the manassas battlefield where he died. Five Forks Cemetery in Pageland holds the grave of James H. Miller, a prisoner of war executed to discourage attacks on Union foragers during Sherman's advance. The other prisoners were required to choose the victim by lot. Miller's headstone reads, "Murdered in retaliation." Sweetwater Cemetery has the grave of the first South Carolinian killed in the war, Private Sidney Weeks.

Rivers Bridge State Park, seven miles west of Ehrhardt off State Route 64 near the Salkehatchie Swamp, preserves relics, breastworks, and Confederate graves where the commander of the 32nd Georgia promised to hold "until next Christmas if you can keep them off my flanks." But the flanks could not be held, and Confederates continued to retreat before Sherman's advance. Elsewhere, memorial plaques identify various incidents, including the battle on the main street of Aiken in February 1865, when Union troops tried to destroy Graniteville Mills. Museums in Lancaster and Mayfield house war relics.

Confederate coastal defenses outside Charleston drew Union attention throughout the war. The occupation of Port Royal

Charleston, one of the South's most attractive cities, had been severely damaged by artillery by war's end, as this 1865 photo shows. The city surrendered to General William T. Sherman when he turned north, after reaching the sea at Savannah, Georgia.

The Parrott gun was one of the most popular cannon used during the Civil War. The rifled weapon, produced in various sizes, was used by both sides. This example is at Fort Gregg on Morris Island, South Carolina in 1865.

Confederate ammunition and arms, stacked near an armory at Charleston, represent only a fraction of the quantities involved. More than 5,000 shells were fired by the two sides during the short siege of the city.

Charleston's South Battery, not too different today, was one of the vantage points from which excited citizens watched the Confederate bombardment of Fort Sumter. As with most early events of the war, an air of festivity prevailed.

Sound and Hilton Head Island was an early achievement of Union arms. Remnants of Confederate Fort Walker, which succumbed to Union naval fire because it was improperly constructed and armed, exist on the posh resort island, which gives little other indication of the isolation and harshness of duty there during the War Between the States. Hilton Head was headquarters of Union Army Department of the South, commanded by Brigadier General Thomas W. Sherman (also known as "The Other" Sherman), and thus a major staging base for the coastal operations in South Carolina, Georgia, and Florida. The ruins of Confederate Fort White, defended successfully against several Federal attacks, are one of the attractions at Belle Island Gardens near Georgetown. During one attack on this fort, the Union flagship, *Harvest Moon*, was sunk by Confederate mines.

The attack on Fort Sumter ignited a civil war that would last four years and cost more lives than any other conflict in American history. More than 8,700 armed clashes, large and small, would be fought in 39 campaigns, which included 76 full-scale battles. The Union would call 2,865,028 men to arms, while the Confederacy, less populous and less industrialized, would muster between 600,000 and 1,000,000. At least 500,000 soldiers, more than 359,000 of them Union men, and untold numbers of civilians would die before the last muster was held on combat fields strewn from Pennsylvania to Arizona. Federal records, while not complete, show 110,070 killed in battle or dying later of wounds, but by far the most thorough killer was disease, which claimed twice as many lives as bullets. Being new organizations, the Confederate military services were even less proficient at keeping records than were their adversaries. The figures often used for Confederate losses — 52,954 in combat, 21,570 of wounds, and 59,279 of disease — seem low because Southerners were aggressive in combat and disease was impartial to the color of the uniform.

States removed from the front would be affected in various, and sometimes unexpected, ways. New York City's mayor at one point proposed that the city and Long Island secede and become a free port, trading with both sides. Rioting broke out in New York City on July 13, 1863, when the drafting of men into military service began, and troops had to be called from the front to put it down. An estimated 1,200 people died. Confederates attempted various schemes to impede the Northern war effort, from disruption of elections in Chicago to an unsuccessful attempt to burn part of New York City. A raid from Canada against St. Albans, Vermont, destroyed a number of buildings and emptied the bank. A Confederate naval group entered the harbor at Portland, Maine, and stole the revenue cutter *Caleb Cushing* but had to burn it when pursued. In Ohio, Southerners burned two steamers on Lake Erie on September 19, 1865, but failed in another part of the plan to free Confederate prisoners near Sandusky. Sites of large Union prison camps set up on islands at Rock Island, Illinois, and in Delaware Bay (in Fort Delaware) remain. And of course the Ford Theater in Washington, D.C., where President Lincoln was assassinated, has been restored as a historical landmark.

Such incidents were sideshows to the main battles precipitated by the attack on Fort Sumter. As the smoke dissipated over Charleston harbor, war clouds were already forming in Virginia in a big way.

VIRGINIA
Manassas (Bull Run)

A stern-faced statue of Major General Thomas J. "Stonewall" Jackson, his taut muscles pressing against his uniform, perpetually surveys the battlefield of Manassas (Bull Run)* from a vantage point on Henry Hill. The statue is a veritable symbol of power, and it stands on the ridge where the Confederate leader during the heat of battle received one of the most famous nicknames in history. But even such a heroic representation does not do justice to that imperturbable, demanding leader who inspired his men to prodigious feats, that superior tactician whose campaigns would later be studied by officers from many nations, yet who believed firmly that, once he had done his best, the outcome of the battle rested in God's hands. Jackson's solidity was crucial to the Confederate victory in the first major land conflict of the War Between the States because, at a critical moment, he provided a rallying point for Southern soldiers who only a few weeks earlier had been plowing fields or toting up accounts.

Manassas National Battlefield Park, 25 miles from the District of Columbia, preserves the scene of two battles fought a little more than a year apart. The first, on July 21, 1861, was the largest ever recorded up to that time in the Western Hemisphere; the second, on August 28–September 1, 1862, was even bigger and paved the way for the first Southern invasion of the North. Confederate success in both instances threatened the national capital. While the second battle did not produce the "firsts" of First Manassas, it was just as important. More than 100,000 troops were involved and 19,514 were killed and wounded — four times the number at the first battle.

This bigger-than-life statue of a stern-faced General Thomas J. Jackson dominates Henry Hill, where his performance in the Battle of First Manassas earned him the nickname "Stonewall."

*The opposing sides in the Civil War frequently gave different names to the same battle. This book employs those currently in use by national or state parks, regardless of origin.

It was inevitable that fighting would occur at Manassas. Virginia had worked for reconciliation between the Union and seceding states until President Lincoln issued a call for 75,000 militia and volunteers to put down the rebellion — then cast her lot with the Confederacy. Her geographic location on the border made her a likely battleground, especially after Richmond became the Confederate capital. The town of Manassas was a transportation hub for the approaches to both Richmond and the fertile Shenandoah Valley; General Robert E. Lee, who had turned down command of United States forces to join his native state and who initially served as adviser to Confederate President Jefferson Davis, immediately recognized the importance of the junction. Federal forces posted there could pose a double threat to Virginia while protecting the national capital, whose safety was one of Lincoln's major concerns.

Neither side was prepared for war, but neither hesitated. The first battle at Manassas aroused the same enthusiasm and confidence, on both sides, that excited the Southerners before Fort Sumter. Federals were so confident of success that they openly boasted of driving Confederate forces back to Richmond. Curious civilians, including some members of Congress, mingled unhindered with the Union army units, often visiting the camps. Many of them brought picnic baskets as though on a holiday, and some of the ladies had finery with them for the victory ball, which was to be held in Alexandria.

Although the first monument to the battle at Manassas was erected in 1865, with four of the Union generals who took part in attendance, preservation of the battlefield did not begin until the twentieth century. Manassas Battlefield Confederate Park, Inc., and the Sons of Confederate Veterans purchased the 128-acre Henry Farm in 1922 and, 16 years later, conveyed it to the United States Government as an "everlasting memorial to the soldiers of the Blue and the Gray." Later acquisitions, including purchase of the 312-acre Brawner Farm in 1985, brought most of the two battlefields within the park's boundaries, or about 3,600 of the 4,500 acres involved.

The national park reflects both battles. Development so far has been connected primarily with the first battle, but the latest acquisition adds much of the territory of the second battle and may in time

After the Battle of First Manassas, Confederate forces occupied positions at Centreville, while the Union built a ring of forts around Washington. The Confederate defenses at Centerville looked like this in 1862.

enable the park service to expand its presentation. Few of the key structures on the battlefield survive. The Stone Bridge across the creek called Bull Run was destroyed several times; it has been reconstructed. The houses around which the fighting swirled were destroyed, then or later, and have been rebuilt. Adjacent to the new Henry House are the 1865 monument to the "patriots who fell at Bull Run" and the grave of Mrs. Judith Carter Henry, the only civilian casualty of the battle. She was an elderly woman who was killed by Union shrapnel after she refused to leave her home. The neat, clean slope of Henry Hill, where the Park Service Visitors' Center is situated, bears little resemblance to the rough terrain over which the armies fought; but the relative compactness of the battlefield permits visitors to reach major features on foot along established trails. The combination of trails and signs, memorials, reconstructions, and strategically placed cannon of that period contribute to a mental picture of the progress of the battles.

Three trails cover the two distinct phases of the Battle of First Manassas. Two paths meander through much of the ground involved in the morning phase on July 21, 1861, which basically involved a Union flanking movement that initiated the fighting while Confederate forces were still forming to attack the Union army near Centreville. A 1.4-mile loop starts at the Stone Bridge across Bull Run, which Confederates defended as a key point in their line. Because Union Brigadier General Erwin McDowell chose a flanking movement across fords of the stream, the bridge became more important as an obstacle to Union retreat than as a prize in the fighting. Confederate Colonel Nathan "Shanks" Evans became one of the unsung heroes of the battle by correctly diagnosing Union movements and moving his forces from the bridge to Matthews Hill to take the first Union assault. The visitors' trail follows Bull Run northward to Farm Ford, a little-known crossing that a loyalist farmer pointed out to Union forces, and then to Matthews Hill, the scene of the principal morning fighting, which pushed Confederate forces back to Henry Hill. The VanPelt farmhouse, used by Colonel Evans as his headquarters, was destroyed by fire in 1932 and the site is covered by woods. A second trail passes important features around Sudley Ford, the principal crossing point for Union forces attempting to flank Confederate defenders of the bridge: the unfinished railroad grade of the Manassas Gap Independent Line, Sudley Road, Sudley Church (where worshippers gathering for church service were surprised to see Federal troops marching by, and which became a Union hospital during the fighting), and the ruins of Sudley Spring. At this ford, on that hot July day, Union soldiers pausing for water caused one of the numerous delays that were to affect the outcome of the battle.

A one-mile self-guided walking tour of Henry Hill starts at the Henry House behind the Visitors' Center. It affords a view of Matthews Hill and covers the ground of the most significant fighting on the afternoon of July 21. Signs and audio message stations describe the seesaw

The Matthews or Stone House was twice engulfed by the fighting at Manassas, when it was used as a hospital, but it survived. Shells embedded in the walls may still be seen.

The Stone Bridge in 1862 (above) and now (below). This bridge provided a lane of retreat for Union forces at both First and Second Manassas, but was destroyed on several occasions. Now restored to its mid–nineteeth-century appearance, it helps visitors follow the events of both battles, fought on the same ground almost a year apart.

fighting on the slope, in which Federal troops made five partly successful assaults only to be driven back each time by rallying Confederates. The trail also visits the Warrenton Turnpike and the Robinson house, which at the time of the fighting was owned by a freed slave. The site of this house provides a spectacular view over Bull Run toward the mountains to the west. The final leg of the trail crosses the eastern edge of Henry Hill, where Jackson was likened to "a stone wall" by General Bee, who is commemorated by a monument on the site where he was fatally wounded.

The "Rebel yell," which would remain a fixture throughout the war, came into being as Beauregard, Jackson, and others brought their troops to an emotional pitch in the late afternoon. The final clash began about 4 P.M. and ended in a rout of the Federals; as McDowell wrote later, "the retreat soon became a rout, and this soon degenerated still further into panic." One who helped create the panic was a firebrand who had been present at the siege of Fort Sumter three months before, an ardent secessionist named Edmund Ruffin. He fired the final shot of the battle at soldiers fleeing across the Stone Bridge.

The flight toward Washington was panicky, with soldiers and civilians mingling on the dusty roads. What had started with such enthusiasm and promise had ended in disaster, and Washington itself was in jeopardy. It was saved by the exhaustion of the Confederate forces, and the uncertainty of Southerners about how their devotion to secession could justify an offensive stance.

No battlefield can preserve the intangibles that affect the outcome of combat. General McDowell's plan to flank the Confederate position was basically sound, but delays in moving units, faulty logistics and preparation, the inexperience of his troops and officers, and bad judgment during the course of battle proved costly. Confederate execution was not perfect, either, but it was better, and the South

possessed more effective intelligence and communications. The deference shown by the senior officer, Brigadier General Joseph E. Johnston, when he arrived on the scene, to General Pierre Gustave Toutant Beauregard, who was familiar with the situation, was unusual in a war where the egos of officers loomed large. After the war, Johnston and Beauregard would duel in print about what happened and its significance.

First Manassas was the first clash in history between two civilian armies. The Confederacy, as a new nation, entered the

war without a professional army but with an officer corps drawn largely from the United States Army; the Union army at the outset had only 16,000 regulars, most of them engaged in protecting the Western frontier or holed up in East Coast forts.

First Manassas was, in a way, an object lesson in the changes taking place in warfare — the emerging preeminence of firepower and maneuver. This first battle would turn on the strategic value of railroads for quick movement of men and supplies and would prove rail's worth in modern warfare. It saw the first use of the telegraph in war, opening a new era in one of the major requirements of combat — communications. In addition, Confederate use of signal flags represented a new form of battlefield communication. Professor Thaddeus Lowe, who already had demonstrated to Union leaders how balloons could provide combat observation, encountered the hazards of the road as his partly inflated ballon snagged on trees along the road to Manassas. His balloon

The Robinson House, which has a spectacular view of Bull Run creek and nearby hills, was owned by a freed slave at the time of the Manassas battles. It survived both, but was destroyed later. The present building was raised in 1926.

Civil War commanders made extensive use of the telegraph in field communications, and often had to construct the lines that linked them to higher headquarters. These Union lines are being built in 1864.

Pontoon bridges played an important role in the Civil War. This crossing of Bull Run in 1862 was a forerunner of more important uses later, including the crossing of the broad Rappahannock River at Fredericksburg by the Union army.

The Federal army made innovative use of observation balloons early in the war, as this 1862 photograph shows. A Union general was the first to use a balloon to direct artillery fire.

A shortage of naval vessels forced the Confederacy to experiment with small, innovative designs such as this torpedo boat.

tracked the movement of Confederate forces after the battle. Balloons would be used often during the early stage of the war, and in May 1862 a Union general became the first to direct artillery fire by signalling from aloft.

More varieties of weapons were used in the Civil War than in any previous conflict. While the Civil War did produce innovations in weapons and tactics — breech-loading rifles, rifled artillery, the first use of machine guns in combat, submarines, land and sea mines and hand grenades, among them — it was also a proving ground for existing technology and thus of considerable interest to the European powers. Military writers in Great Britain, France, and Germany would recognize it as the first total war, fought with the might produced by the Industrial Revolution, and a glimpse of the warfare of the future. Well into the twentieth century, military authors would draw on the tactical improvisations of Confederate and Union

generals and the prodigious engineering feats performed by both sides.

First Manassas also produced the first winner of the Congressional Medal of Honor, an award created during the Civil War. Although he would not receive it until 33 years later, Adelbert Ames of East Thomaston, Maine, commanding an artillery section, became the first to be named for the honor.

Second Manassas was not a rerun of the first battle, although it involved much of the same terrain. While the first had a carnival air about it, the second was a serious contest between grim-faced veterans who saw no glory in war but still believed in their causes. The first battle was an isolated event expected to end the war quickly; the second was part of an ongoing campaign that followed the failure of Major General George B. McClellan's

This Rodman gun at Alexandria helped strengthen the ring of earthen forts around the District of Columbia. They were never successfully attacked, but only Alexandria's Fort Ward is preserved.

Peninsula campaign. It would prove the genius of Confederate General Robert E. Lee in developing strategy as well as tactics and in using deception, and would reveal his reluctance to impose his will on others, including recalcitrant generals.

Confronted with the threat to Richmond posed by the Peninsula campaign (see chapter 4), Confederate forces had pulled back from northern Virginia. Thus, the new Union Army of Virginia under Major General John Pope, numbering 45,000 men, pushed forward to the Rappahannock and Rapidan Rivers in an attempt to reach Richmond. General McClellan's refusal, after a severe pounding by Lee, to attack Richmond without major reinforcements led to abandonment of the Peninsula campaign and to Lee's decision to attack Pope before the two Union armies could unite. Jackson's division struck Pope's forces in the neat farmlands near Cedar Mountain five miles south of Culpeper just off present U.S. Route 15. The owner of the battleground makes it available each year for a reenactment of the bloody attacks of both sides on the Sunday nearest the August 9 anniversary. The reenactment is under sponsorship of the Culpeper Cavalry Museum, a repository of Civil War relics. (Earthworks on the mountain, also on private property, are from a later period.) Jackson had won

the Battle of Cedar Mountain by the time Lee arrived with fresh forces. Lee then used Jackson's well-known "foot cavalry", augmented by additional units, as though it were horse cavalry, sending Jackson with 24,000 men to destroy Pope's communications with Washington. Lee, with the main body, would follow and unite with Jackson to trap Pope.

It all came together on almost the same spot where the Battle of First Manassas had been fought. Pope, believing he faced only Jackson, threw caution to the winds in an effort to defeat the famous Confederate general and then mistook a tactical withdrawal for retreat. In sending his forces to pursue Jackson, he was committing his army to the second battle of Manassas.

Several places along the Warrenton Turnpike (now U.S. Route 29) and State Routes 234 and 622, within Manassas National Battlefield Park, identify key features of the second battle, which put Union and Confederate forces in positions the reverse of their first encounter. Trails lead to other points of interest, including the strong position behind the unfinished railroad grade, still partly visible in wooded areas, which Jackson defended until Lee's arrival. The heaviest Union assault occurred at a point known as the Deep Cut. Other features include the Stone House,

Union General John Pope was so confident at the Battle of Second Manassas that he mistook a realignment of Confederate forces for retreat and claimed a victory. The next day, he was decisively defeated.

The colorful uniforms that prevailed on both sides at the start of the war, such as those worn by this reactivated Zouaves unit at a modern-day encampment at Culpeper, soon gave way to more practical garb. Encampments re-enact battles and recreate the lifestyles of the soldiers of both armies.

used as a hospital by both sides at different times; Groveton Confederate Cemetery, where only 40 of 200 buried there have been identified; Chinn Ridge and Henry Hill, where stubborn Union resistance prevented a complete rout; the Stone Bridge, across which Federal troops once again retreated; and a memorial to Fletcher Webster, grandson of Daniel Webster, who died leading the 12th Massachusetts Infantry.

Living history programs and battle reenactments recapture some of the drama created when Pope threw Federal units piecemeal against Jackson's front, bending it but never breaking it. Jackson's veterans, low on ammunition, threw rocks to help repel one attack. The arrival of forces under Lee formed a V-shaped line with a 160-degree angle. Major General James "Old Pete" Longstreet's masterful use of artillery to support Jackson marked a turning point in the fighting, and when the Confederate wings moved forward they carried everything before them. This time, it was Union soldiers who held fast on Henry Hill, and their stubborn resistance provided the time for Pope's beaten army to retreat over Bull Run to the prepared defenses at Centreville.

Behind the Centreville line, the District of Columbia was defended by a ring of 68 forts, most of them like the strong earthworks in Alexandria's Fort Ward Park.

Groveton Cemetery holds the remains of 200 Confederate soldiers killed at Manassas, all but 40 of them unknown. Nearby Dogan House is the only structure remaining from the village that existed at the time of the Civil War. 228.

There each year now, the Blue and the Gray collide in a repeat of the 1864 Battle of Fort Stevens, the only Confederate attack on these defenses of Washington. President Lincoln watched the action from behind Union lines — one of the few times in history that an American president came under fire while in office. Fort Myers, the only one of the forts to become permanent, is without Civil War relics.

Not far away is the world-famous Arlington National Cemetery, with graves dating from the Civil War to the present and including those of Unknown Soldiers of twentieth-century wars. The Lee-Custis Mansion, which occupies a prominent hilltop site and is decorated in period style, was the home of General Lee before the Civil War.

Leesburg, in a salient north of Washington and strongly pro-Southern, was the scene of several skirmishes, but no battlefield is preserved. The city retains many

Handsome Arlington House, shown here in 1864, was the home of General Robert E. Lee prior to the outbreak of the Civil War. Located in what is now the national cemetery, it is maintained as an historic site furnished with antiques.

of the buildings prominent in the period, however. A small Union cemetery and two stone monuments are near Dulles International Airport at Ball's Bluff, the site of an early Union disaster that cost hundreds of lives.

The battles at Manassas were largely tactical. Future contests would grow in size, destructiveness, and bitterness.

Confederates, short of cannon, attempted to fool their opponents by siting fake guns, as here at Centreville in 1862. Called "Quaker guns" because of their peaceful nature, they were usually made of wooden logs.

Tiny Centreville, between Washington, D.C. and Manassas, was a key Union position during both Manassas battles. This 1862 photograph shows Union soldiers on the edge of town.

VIRGINIA

The Rappahannock Line

A
Great Battle Going On" declared a headline in *The Washington Star* on December 13, 1862. And indeed it was — but not from the Union standpoint. The Battle of Fredericksburg, which initiated a series of engagements along the Rappahannock River barrier almost halfway between Washington and Richmond, was such a disaster that it was the only one Major General Ambrose E. Burnside would lead as commander of the Army of the Potomac.

Burnside did not want the command because he lacked experience. President Lincoln had doubts, too, but they were overcome by his exasperation at the slow movement of General George B. McClellan, who had allowed Lee to withdraw his army uncontested from Maryland after the inconclusive Battle of Antietam. Burnside must have been influenced by Lincoln's impatience, for he pushed into hostile territory in wintertime and persisted in following his plan of attack even when confronted by General Robert E. Lee in possession of one of the most naturally defensible positions used in the Civil War: Marye's Heights and adjacent hills south of Fredericksburg.

The opening phase of the Battle of Fredericksburg might have been an omen for Burnside. Confederate sharpshooters hidden in the historic and until then peaceable city of less than 5,000 inhabitants prevented his engineers from completing pontoon bridges across the river — one of the innovations associated with the battle — even after he had devasted the town with artillery. Only by using his pontoons in the manner of landing craft — another innovation that anticipated modern warfare — was he able to push enough forces across the river to clear the city of snipers and skirmishers. The worst was yet to come.

General Ambrose E. Burnside commanded the Union attack at Fredericksburg, broken by Lee's masterful defense of Marye's Heights.

The scene today is quite different from what his soldiers saw as they moved through the narrow streets of the city, sometimes having to clear a street block by block, to the snow-covered fields and heights. Fredericksburg has gown to incorporate the area of the December 13, 1862, battle; only essential parts of the battlefield have been preserved. These are divided into three units, starting with a walking tour from the Visitors' Center along the base of Marye's Heights, where Confederates entrenched behind the stone wall at the Sunken Road mowed down Union lines attacking across open fields. The tour also passes the remains of the home of Martha Stevens, the "heroine of the battle of Fredericksburg" who stayed in her house to tend the wounded; her grave, whose marker recounts her death almost 26 years to the day after the battle; a cottage known as the Innis House, which survived even though it was used as a shelter by Confederate sharpshooters; and a monument to "The Angel of Marye's Heights," Richard Rowland Kirkland, a South Caroilina soldier who risked his life to bring water to the thirsty wounded of both sides.

The second unit of the battlefield park is the terraced national cemetery on Marye's Heights, where more than 15,000 Union troops are buried amid memorials to many of the units that took part. Near the entrance, a tall column bearing an iron cross, erected by Major General Daniel Butterfield, commemorates the valor of the Union V Corps and its 35,708 members who died during the course of the war. On the crest of the hill, from which Louisiana's Washington Battery and other artillery units raked the attacking Union army, the 127th Regiment of the Pennsylvania Infantry is commemorated. The view from the cemetery shows how the heights command the surrounding terrain. The combination of strategically placed cannon firing from the hill and infantry shooting from the Stone Wall was so effective that Colonel E.P. Alexander boasted, "A chick-

en could not live on that field." A second assault, east of Marye's Heights, should have been coordinated with the main effort but wasn't, and was also beaten back by Lee's triumphant forces.

The third unit of the battlefield park is a self-drive tour that begins at the base of Lee Hill, the vantage point from which the Confederate commander watched the battle. It was there, when it became obvious that victory would be complete, that Lee allowed himself a little show of ebullience: "It is well that war is so terri-

Confederate dead lie neatly on the Sunken Road after the Battle of Fredericksburg. Although Confederates behind the Stone Wall mowed down the attacking Federals, their losses were heavy.

General Robert E. Lee was the South's most famous general. Lee in command was like another army in the field, according to one historian.

"The Angel of Marye's Heights," Sergeant Richard R. Kirkland, is memorialized by this monument near the base of the hill. The Confederate soldier risked his life to carry water to the thirsty wounded of both sides.

ble — we should grow too fond of it," he said. Other features on the eight-mile drive (12 miles back to the Visitors' Center) through wooded terrain are a well-preserved section of Confederate infantry trench; the point where Major General George G. Meade's Federals briefly pierced the Confederate line; and the Confederate artillery strongpoints of Prospect Hill and Major John Pelham's Position, still fortified with cannon of that time.

ERECTED BY
THE STATE OF SOUTH CAROLINA
THE COMMONWEALTH OF VIRGINIA
COLLATERAL DESCENDANTS OF
RICHARD KIRKLAND AND
CITIZENS OF THE UNITED STATES

DR. RICHARD NUNN LANIER
EXECUTIVE DIRECTOR
OF THE

IN MEMORIAM
RICHARD ROWLAND KIRKLAND
CO. G, 2ND SOUTH CAROLINA VOLUNTEERS
C.S.A.

AT THE RISK OF HIS LIFE THIS AMERICAN
SOLDIER OF SUBLIME COMPASSION BROUGHT
WATER TO HIS WOUNDED FOES AT
FREDERICKSBURG. THE FIGHTING MEN ON
BOTH SIDES OF THE LINE CALLED HIM

Confederates on the heights outside Fredericksburg were attacked again the following spring, and this time Union forces were successful against a thin gray line. The battle was secondary to the main fighting around Chancellorsville, 10 miles away, however.

Chancellorsville is regarded as Lee's most masterful battle, but it was a costly one because it resulted in the death of Thomas J. "Stonewall" Jackson. Relics of the battle are strung out along State Route 3 (the Orange Turnpike) west of Fredericksburg, but many features of the battlefield are within the national park. The Visitors' Center is situated on ground where major fighting took place. It is more important in this park than in most others because the circular driving tour does not portray adequately the master strokes that achieved another Confederate victory against far superior Union forces holding

More than 15,000 Union soldiers lie among the memorials in the national cemetery on Marye's Heights. From this vantage point, Confederate artillery poured cross and frontal fire onto Union attackers below, with devasting effect.

From this hilltop, now decorated with cannon, General Lee watched the progress of the Battle of Fredericksburg.

A burial detail completes its grisly task after the Wilderness Campaign in 1864. The scene became commonplace as losses mounted during General Ulysses S. Grant's push into Virginia.

strong positions. The background a visitor obtains from a 12-minute slide presentation and the center's excellent museum will add meaning to later stops at Hazel Grove (now fortified with a few of the three dozen Confederate cannon crowded there at the time), as will a painting, depicting the artillery duel with massed Union cannon at Fairview, to the trenches and earthworks visible at both sites. Even the foundations of Chancellorsville Tavern, which gave the battle its name, will seem more evocative.

In a way, the Battle of Chancellorsville was a follow-up to the Union defeat at Fredericksburg the previous December. Major General Joseph "Fighting Joe" Hooker, who succeeded Burnside as commander of the Union's 130,000-man Army of the Potomac, made his winter camp near Fredericksburg and resumed the "On to Richmond" drive in the spring. With the lesson of the futile attack on Marye's Heights burned into his mind, Hooker chose to combine a flanking movement against Lee with a new assault on the hills south of Fredericksburg. Lee anticipated his plan, though, and although outnumbered nearly three to one took the initiative on May 1. Hooker's units fell back from positions that were crucial to the outcome of the battle. In this wooded countryside, Hazel Grove was one of the

few open places where cannon had clear fields of fire. But the key to success was Stonewall Jackson's brilliant surprise flank attack that collapsed the right wing of Hooker's army. Jackson's winding march from the bivouac where he and Lee had agreed on the tactic can be duplicated by following the Furnace Road and the Jackson Trail (part of it unpaved) to State Routes 613 and 3.

Jackson was determined to push his success the next day; so he rode out at night with a small staff to reconnoiter. The group was mistaken for enemy on their return and Jackson was badly wounded in the left arm, which was amputated in the field. The loss of Jackson was serious, but the next morning Lee threw his army against the fortified Union line, driving Hooker back to new positions a mile north of Chancellorsville.

The thin gray Confederate line left to defend the heights near Fredericksburg had been breached by Federals, however, and Lee was forced to split his army once again. At Salem Church, seven miles east of Chancellorsville (now restored as part of the battlefield park), the reinforced Confederates halted this Union drive and pushed it back across the Rappahannock River.

Meanwhile, the wounded Jackson was taken 27 miles to T.C. Chandler's Fairfield

Plantation at Guiney (now Guinea) Station, a key supply center on the Richmond, Fredericksburg and Potomac Railway line, where it was thought he could receive proper care. The main house was already filled with wounded from the fighting, and so Jackson was placed in the nearby white frame plantation office. The days that followed were marked alternately with optimism and despair as pneumonia set in. On the afternoon of May 10, eight days after his greatest victory, Jackson became delirious and began shouting military commands. That subsided into silence, and then he drew on his knowledge of the Bible as he said, "Let us cross over the river, and rest under the shade of the trees."

Death had claimed the general Lee had called his right arm; Lee would miss Jack-

son sorely in the battles to come. Many years later David Lloyd George, the British statesman, would remark, "In this little house, the Confederacy also died." The small wooden building where Stonewall died is the main feature of the Jackson Shrine, which is five miles off Interstate 95 via State Routes 606 and 607. It is furnished plainly inside, with the original bed and blanket and clock (which still works) on the mantelshelf. Another room is outfitted as the doctor's room. A painting, with a recorded commentary, at the entrance to the small park depicts the plantation at the time of Jackson's death. Only the foundations of the brick manor house remain.

On June 9, 1863, the Rappahannock line witnessed the greatest cavalry battle of the war when more than 10,000 riders

The wounded at Chancellorsville were treated at field stations. More seriously wounded men were taken to field hospitals, which usually occupied a nearby farmhouse. Despite advances during the war, military medical practice remained primitive on both sides.

General Joseph "Fighting Joe" Hooker commanded the Union army at Chancellorsville.

The Stonewall Jackson Shrine at Guinea Station preserves the plantation office in which Lee's "right arm" died as a result of wounds received at Chancellorsville. The manor house, also used as a Confederate hospital, no longer exists.

clashed at Brandy Station, five miles north of Culpeper, as a preliminary to the battle at Gettysburg. The site looks much as it did during the 12-hour battle, but is undeveloped, with only an historical marker.

It was 1864 when Lee met General Ulysses S. Grant on the field of battle for the first time. The Wilderness Battlefield, part of the battleground complex around Fredericksburg, preserves the site where Grant, as General-in-Chief of all Union armies, began the costly strike-and-flank campaign of attrition that would end the war. A drive around the portion of the battlefield owned by the park service shows why the dense thickets and tangled overgrowth earned the name Wilderness, and why the fighting was so confused that whole units became lost. Heavy firing set fire to dry underbrush, too, adding to the confusion.

The national park lies roughly south of State Route 20, approximately the same route along which Lee moved part of his forces to meet Grant. The Wilderness Exhibit Center has paintings and written commentaries on the battle, and the road through the park passes landmark farms and remnants of Confederate trenches dug for the battle of May 5–6, 1864. A monument to Hood's Texans, who fought at the Wilderness as part of Longstreet's Corps, recalls an incident that formed a bond betwen Lee and the Texans in the Army of Northern Virginia, one that would outlive the war. At a critical point in the fighting near the Widow Trapp Farm, Lee determined to rally his forces by leading a charge himself. The Texans there were appalled, and shouted to Lee that they would not go unless he moved back to safety.

General Thomas J. "Stonewall" Jackson pushed his men, but shared their hardships. His Stonewall Brigade continued to serve with distinction after his death.

*This Kurz & Allison print
depicts the struggle for
Laurel Hill at Spotsylvania,
where dismounted
Confederate cavalry held
off superior Union forces
until Lee could once again
place his army between
General Grant and
Richmond.*

*General George G. Meade
set up his headquarters at
Culpeper in 1863.*

"Go back, General, go back!" shouted the Texans.

"Hooray for Texas!" shouted Lee, waving his hat.

Lee retreated, and the Texans charged. This was not the first time Confederate soldiers had been concerned for their leaders, but ever afterward Lee retained a special affection for the Texans under his command.

The Wilderness battle was a draw. The Federals abandoned the field, but this time they did not retreat across the Rappahannock River. They turned southward in another flanking movement that would renew the fighting at Spotsylvania Courthouse. From the Wilderness the drive follows the Brock Road (State Route 613), along which many Federal troops walked, and turns onto Grant Drive at the entrance to the park.

There is a good view from the exhibit shelter of the Laurel Hill area, where on May 8, 1864, dismounted Confederate cavalrymen fought a determined holding action against a superior Federal force until Confederate infantrymen, hastening from the Wilderness, reinforced them and put Lee once again between Grant and Richmond. Paintings and commentaries at and near the shelter provide a good introduction to both the seven-mile walking tour of the battlefield, which begins there, and the drive through the park. The principal feature of this park is the Bloody Angle, a salient where the firing was so heavy that it severed the trunk of an oak tree 22 inches thick. Monuments to New Jersey, New York, and Ohio troops who assaulted the salient, and a walking trail, now occupy the site where some of the most savage hand-to-hand fighting of the war occurred. At the McCoull House within the salient, Lee once again prepared to lead a charge but was dissuaded by Virginians and Georgians. The incredible bravery displayed by soldiers on both sides did not determine the outcome at the Bloody Angle; not until a new line had been prepared across the base of the salient did the Confederates pull back to Lee's last line, almost parallel to Brock Road. A strong Union assault on this line was crushed by infantry and 30 massed cannon.

Sporadic fighting went on around Spotsylvania Courthouse for almost two weeks, and the battle cost Grant 18,000 men. The number of Southern casualties is unknown, but some of those killed are buried in the Confederate Cemetery off State Route 208 east of Spotsylvania. The battle was another draw, and Grant again abandoned the field to maneuver southward. More bloody battles in the war of attrition lay ahead; the war was still far from being over.

VIRGINIA
Richmond and The End

O
n to Richmond!" was the Union's battle cry in the east, but it was easier said than done. In their fortified line around Washington, Federal forces were only a hundred miles from the Confederate capital over easy terrain with good roads. After First Manassas, though, it might as well have been the moon. The initial optimism gave way to resolve, and President Lincoln chose General George B. McClellan to build and field a Union army that could take Richmond. "Little Mac" was better at building than at marching; he devised a strategy for indirect action that would force the South to submit after he gained control of strategic railroad junctions.

After much prodding by Lincoln, McClellan set in motion a plan to approach Richmond indirectly through the Virginia Peninsula, a historic sliver of land lying between the James and York rivers. This campaign, sandwiched between the two battles at Manassas, was an attempt to follow a line of least resistance. His success at turning the rabble that had run at First Manassas into the well-schooled and disciplined Army of the Potomac encouraged even the hesitant McClellan. But when his army of 150,000 was reduced to 105,000 men — Lincoln insisted on retaining 37,000 men, formed into the Army of Virginia, to defend Washington — optimism was short-lived. He would consistently, in this campaign and others, overestimate the size of the forces opposing him and doubt he had enough men of his own.

McClellan's Peninsula campaign had certain advantages. The rivers and Fortress (now Fort) Monroe in Hampton at the tip of the Peninsula provided secure supply lines and protected his flanks. The route reduced the distance on land to Richmond by 30 miles and was only lightly defended at the time he formulated his plan. Defensive lines at Yorktown and Williamsburg could be bypassed by river with the cooperation of the Navy.

Virginia had not captured Fortress Monroe, which, like Fort Sumter, was part of the coastal defenses constructed after the War of 1812. The Confederacy exercised nominal control over the adjacent land area — the citizens of Hampton, the

additions to accommodate Coast Artillery. Although still an active garrison today as headquarters of the Army's Training and Doctrine Command, the historic aspects of the moated, star-shaped brick and stone fort are open to the public. These include casemates (rooms in the walls of the fort), which house the museum preserving the small cell in which Jefferson Davis was imprisoned after the war. The Casemate

Fortress (now Fort) Monroe, held throughout the war by the Union, has ties with both President Abraham Lincoln and Confederate President Jefferson Davis. Lincoln stayed in Quarters 1 during a wartime visit; the cell where Davis was imprisoned after the war is now part of the Casemate Museum.

nearest community, burned their city rather than surrender it to Union forces — but fortified a line of trenches and forts anchored on Yorktown and extending across the Peninsula. These had withstood an early probe by Brigadier General Benjamin Butler and delayed McClellan's advance until General Joseph E. Johnston could bring 60,000 troops south from his Manassas line. Johnston's fighting retreat along the Peninsula included a one-day battle at Williamsburg, which enabled the bulk of his forces to settle into positions before Richmond.

Fort Monroe, completed in 1834, remains an outstanding example of a mid-nineteenth-century citadel despite later

Museum also explores the development of coast artillery and the first battle of ironclad ships, which took place in Hampton Roads. Lincoln stayed in the large white frame building directly in front of the main entrance, known as Quarters 1, during a visit to the fort in May 1862. Robert E. Lee's prewar quarters, where he lived when he was a young lieutenant of engineers while directing work on Fortress Monroe and Fort Wool (a much-changed fort on an island offshore), also are identified. The large parade ground is decorated with a 15-inch Rodman gun known as the Lincoln Cannon.

The first land battle of the war occurred in 1861 in Hampton when 4,000 untested

*This watercolor (right)
from the National Archives
of Union headquarters near
Yorktown in April of 1862
probably gives an idealized
picture, but it shows the
conditions under which
command decisions were
made in the field.*

*The Lincoln gun (below), a
15-inch Rodman used
during the war, was named
to honor the president's
visit to Fort Monroe. Now
dismounted, it overlooks the
large parade ground of the
still-active military post.*

Federals failed to dislodge 1,500 equally green Confederates at Big Bethel. The first battle casualty of the war was Henry Lawson Wyatt of North Carolina, whose statue stands on the grounds of the Old Capitol in Raleigh, N.C.

Some of the fortifications raised at Yorktown during the Civil War are incorporated into the layout of the Yorktown battlefield, where American independence was won during the Revolutionary War. The eroded breastworks in Newport News Park were part of the imaginative line, incorporating dams, built by Confederate Colonel John B. Magruder and are among the best preserved fortifications in Virginia. History trails and a painting recount the fighting in the area. There are additional (unrestored) breastworks at Wynn's Mill, some distance from the main park area.

At sea, Union forces already had implemented a version of the Anaconda Plan, which called for occupation of the key points along the coast of the Confederacy. The Northern blockade, proclaimed by Lincoln on April 19, less than a week after the fall of Fort Sumter, slowly strangled the foreign trade of the Confederacy and caused privation and hardship among soldiers and civilians alike. Breaking the blockade became a necessity for the South.

South and North both experimented with ironclad vessels, and the inventions of the two sides met off the coast of Virginia on March 9, 1862, in Hampton Roads. The C.S.S. *Virginia* incorporated the hull of the U.S.S. *Merrimac*, which had burned to the waterline when the Union evacuated Norfolk in April 1861; her new above-water structure was plated with two inches of armor. The *Monitor*, in contrast, had been built in New York according to a radical design developed by an inventor named John Ericsson.

Its first day out of Norfolk, the C.S.S. *Virginia* had a field day against the wooden Federal warships anchored off Newport News, sinking the sloop *Cumberland* (part of its anchor chain is on display at Casino Park in Newport News) and destroying the grounded frigate *Congress*. The consternation among Federal naval and army officers exceeded the damage caused by the fighting; unchallenged, the *Virginia* could endanger the Union position on the Peninsula and break the blockade. The arrival of Ericsson's *Monitor* that night brought great relief, and the two iron monsters steamed out the following morning to write naval history in the first battle of ironclad warships.

The contest was a draw: The *Virginia* was slow, unwieldy, and her draft was too great for shallow water; the *Monitor* was unwieldy, too, had difficulty with her guns and equipment, and was subject to flood-ing. At the end of the day, the *Monitor* was anchored under the protective guns of Fort Monroe and the *Virginia* had returned to Norfolk.

They did not meet again. Although the existence of the *Virginia* inhibited for a while McClellan's use of the James River in his Peninsula campaign, both ships ended ingloriously. The *Virginia* was sunk to prevent her capture when Norfolk was evacuated by Confederate forces only two months after the historic sea duel, and the *Monitor* sank in a storm off Cape Hatteras. Numerous efforts to find the *Monitor* failed until, in 1973, modern technology spotted the vessel on the bottom of the ocean. Although there has been discussion about raising the vessel, only a few pieces have been recovered.

The story of the *Monitor–Virginia* (or *Merrimac*) battle is told at both the Casemate Museum at Fort Monroe and the

The battle between the **Monitor** *(sometimes derisively called a "cheesebox on a raft") and the* **Virginia** *continued for four hours but ended inconclusively, with neither ironclad seriously damaged.*

This photograph of the deck of the **Monitor** *after the battle with the* **Virginia** *clearly shows dented armor plate, but no major damage from the close-quarters, hard-fought battle.*

The sunken wreck of the **Monitor** *was located in 1973, but it was not until recently that clear photographs could be taken. This shot shows a gun port in the turret.*

Yorktown (right), where American independence was won during the Revolutionary War, also was an important Confederate defensive position during the Civil War.

Mariners' Museum in Newport News. Tour boats in Hampton Roads pass through the area in which they fought, although the tours concentrate more on the modern naval and commercial ships in the nation's largest natural harbor and on shoreline installations such as the Newport News shipyard, which builds nuclear warships.

Like Manassas, Richmond is a multiple battlefield. The Confederate capital was the principal objective of seven Union drives and was besieged on two occasions: The first was the unsuccessful Peninsula campaign; the second was part of Ulysses S. Grant's continuing operations that would lead to Lee's surrender at Appomattox. As a result, Richmond Battlefield National Park brings together a number of battle sites associated with two campaigns.

The park's headquarters are in a former weather-bureau building in Chimborazo Park in Richmond. A museum and an audiovisual show about the confusing series of actions make this a good place to begin a tour of the battlefield park. The tour follows highways in a rough arc east of the city. Additional Visitors' Centers are at Cold Harbor, northeast of the city, and at Fort Harrison, to the south.

The fighting for Richmond began at Fair Oaks (on State Route 33) on May 31, 1862. The intensity of the Seven Days' Campaign that followed can be seen in the national cemetery at nearby Seven Pines, on the Williamsburg Road (U.S. Route 60). General Johnston was wounded in his attack on McClellan, and General Robert E. Lee replaced him. This was one of the most significant events of the war; as one historian has said, having Lee in command was worth another army in the field.

McClellan's army was close enough to hear the church bells ringing in Richmond. Lee took the initiative on June 26 with an imaginative and daring plan. McClellan's forces were divided by the rain-swollen Chickahominy River and this made his right flank, under Brigadier General Fitz-John Porter, vulnerable.

Overlooks in the Mechanicsville area northeast of Richmond show the area where Lee's assault began. Lee himself watched the initial phase of the battle from near the Chickahominy Bluff overlook, just off present U.S. Route 360 (Mechanicsville Road). Remnants of Union defenses remain at Beaver Dam Creek, where massed artillery and musket fire halted the Confederate attack. At Gaines Mill, scene of most of the fighting on the second day, vestiges of shallow Union trenches are visible along the nature trail to Breakthrough Point.

In his first action, Lee used many of the tactics he would employ throughout the remainder of the war. He left a light defensive force between the main enemy army and Richmond and sent the remainder of his army, together with Stonewall Jackson's troops brought secretly from the Valley, against the vulnerable flank. Delays prevented Jackson from arriving in time for the first battle, and the stiff resistance of Porter's units kept Lee from achieving his objective. Nevertheless, Porter's orderly withdrawal began the retrograde action that would take McClellan to the banks of the James River at Harrison's Landing on Berkeley Plantation, from which the Northern army would ultimately be withdrawn on the eve of Second Manassas. The army, camped under the protection of the Union fleet in the river, left more than the minié-balls and knapsack buckles that enthusiasts hunt for nowadays with metal detectors after spring planting; it was during this time that General Butterfield wrote the haunting bugle call, "Taps". McClellan used the eighteenth-century Berkeley mansion as his headquarters, a use that is overshadowed by the other historical aspects of the mansion: It is the ancestral home of the Harrison family, which produced a signer of the Declaration of Independence and two presidents and is now owned by a descendant of a Union bugler who participated in the campaign.

Cold Harbor, a few miles from Mechanicsville, two years later (in June 1864) would become one of the bloodiest battlefields of the war as General Grant maintained his grinding war of attrition on

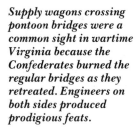

Supply wagons crossing pontoon bridges were a common sight in wartime Virginia because the Confederates burned the regular bridges as they retreated. Engineers on both sides produced prodigious feats.

Confederate forces. In one 30-minute period, the Army of the Potomac sustained 7,000 casualties assaulting Confederate defenses. The battlefield area within the national park has good examples of the types of earthworks raised by the Confederates, which originally stretched for six miles. A path leads through the works and over small connecting bridges. Other major features are the Gathright House, the Watt House, and walking trails with interpretive signs.

Malvern Hill, closer to the James River than the Chickahominy, was the last of the Seven Days' battles. The battlefield is well preserved, and cannon of that period stand by a visitors' center on the crest of the slight rise that Union forces defended, standing upright against a frontal assault. Confederates advancing across the open field were pushed together by the lay of the land and mown down by concentrated artillery and musket fire.

The string of forts west of Malvern Hill combines the actions of two separate battles. Drewry's Bluff, or Fort Darling, was a Confederate strongpoint on the James River south of Richmond. Exhibits and markers at the scenic site provide an account of the unsuccessful attack on the fort in 1862 by four Union gunboats, including the ironclad *Monitor*, and a revenue steamer. Fort Brady was constructed by the Union to neutralize Drewry's Bluff. Fort Harrison, the largest and best preserved, was built by the Confederates and enlarged and strengthened by the Federals after they captured it in 1864. A footpath through the fort and visual displays show the unusual design of the fortress, which was divided into segments to minimize shell bursts. The smaller Fort Gilmore, although heavily attacked, remained in Confederate hands until Richmond was evacuated. Even smaller Fort Hoke became a strategic strongpoint.

Parker's Battery was a Confederate artillery strongpoint that helped immobilize General Benjamin F. Butler's Army of the James in 1864. Hopewell, east of Rich-

mond on the James River, was called City Point in those days. Its strategic location is recognized by the remains of Fort Abbott.

The battle for Richmond was finally fought at Petersburg, an important rail and highway center 25 miles south of the Confederate capital. Petersburg National Battlefield's 1,531 acres preserve relics of all the phases of the 10-month siege of the city, which brought great hardship to Confederate soldiers and Petersburg civilians alike and proved the overwhelming industrial and financial capacity of the North.

Unsuccessful in direct assaults on Richmond, Grant resumed his efforts to outflank Lee and cut off his communications to the south and west. His initial attack on Petersburg was successful. Even though the Dimmock Line had been constructed after the Peninsula campaign, it was too lightly manned. Battery 5, at the rear of the park Visitors' Center, was one of nine original strongpoints in the line. It is a good example of the earthworks fort used in the war and is outfitted with cannon of that era. Nearby, in a shaded glen, is the "Dictator", replica of the 2,000-pound

Federal mortar that was used to lob 200-pound explosive shells into Petersburg, then 2.5 miles away.

Fort Stedman, the scene of Lee's desperate attempt to break Grant's siege, is now shaded by trees and visited by boys shouting "Bang, bang" as they climb on the

(Overleaf top) Union soldiers, mostly miners from Pennsylvania, dug a tunnel under the Confederate line at Petersburg in an effort to breach it. Remnants of the tunnel remain.

(Overleaf bottom) The weathered, grass-covered Crater is not as impressive now as it was in 1865, but it is one of the main features of Petersburg National Battlefield Park. Then, it was a gaping hole into which 15,000 Union troops rushed, only to be trapped by a Confederate counterattack. The action resulted in 5,500 casualties, 4,000 of them Union.

The big guns at Drewry's Bluff, called Fort Darling by the Union, dominated the James River south of Richmond so completely that even an attack by Union ironclads was beaten off.

cannon. A nearby painting shows a different scene in 1865 — well-defended raw earthworks against which Confederate units are being hurled, only to be forced back by superior forces.

The Crater, the best-known feature of the battlefield, recalls an incident that, tragic though it was, had little effect on the war. There are remnants of a tunnel dug by men of the 48th Pennsylvania Infantry Regiment, many of them coal miners in civilian life, and of the crater created when 8,000 pounds of black powder exploded under the Confederate strongpoint known as Elliott's Salient. Fifteen thousand Federal troops attacked through and around the gaping, smoking hole in the ground that had destroyed more than a hundred feet of the Confederate line; but many were trapped as a Confederate counterattack, led by Major General William Mahone, forced them back into the crater. By the time it was over, 5,500 men had been killed, wounded or captured, 4,000 of them Federals. Ironically, the Confederates had suspected something was afoot and dug an exploratory tunnel themselves, missing the Union tunnel by only a few feet.

Petersburg Battlefield has other outstanding relics, including Battery 9, which was captured by black troops, and Meade Station, an important supply point for Grant's army. A replica of an earthworks system complete with log structures and trenches, situated at the entrance to this stop on the self-drive tour of the battlefield, gives a good indication of how primitive life in the field was.

Grant's superiority in manpower, transportation, and logistics decided the battle for Petersburg — and the fate of the Army of Northern Virginia. As Grant lengthened his lines, Lee's forces were stretched thinner and thinner. Grant began to cut the rail and road approaches to Petersburg from the south, one by one, and a final assault on April 2, 1865, compelled Lee to abandon Petersburg. Confederate President Davis received the sad news while

The Gathright House (above left), a short distance from Cold Harbor, was used as a hospital during the bloodiest half-hour of the war. A frontal assault cost Grant 7,000 casualties.

The restored Watt House (above right) is a landmark of the 1862 Battle of Gaines Mill near Richmond. Remnants of Union trenches breached by attacking Texans and Georgians remain nearby.

Fort Harrison, built by the Confederates and strengthened and enlarged by the Union after its capture, is an excellent example of an earthen Civil War fort.

attending church in Richmond's St. Paul's Episcopal Church. The event is recalled by pew plaques and the Lee memorial window.

The day would become even sadder for the Confederacy: People who for the most part had borne up well under years of danger and months of siege went wild as the Confederate army began pulling out. To prevent violence, whiskey barrels were emptied into the steets; but people scooped it up in pails and sopped it up with cloths. Distribution of food in the government commissary turned into a near riot. An attempt to burn the tobacco at Shockoe Slip to keep it from falling into Union hands set the city ablaze. The fire spread unchecked until Union forces entered the city and demolished buildings to create fire breaks. Shockoe Slip was reborn after the war as an industrial zone, but today it is mainly a chic area of restaurants and specialty shops.

Like Charleston, Richmond has many places that recall the War Between the States. In the State Capitol, whose central

building was designed by Thomas Jefferson, the Confederate Congress met. General Lee received command of the Virginia forces there. Statues in Capitol Square memorialize "Stonewall" Jackson, one of Virginia's governors during the Civil War, and Dr. Hunter McGuire, Confederate surgeon.

The White House of the Confederacy, Jefferson Davis's residence when he was President, is incorporated into the Confederate Museum. This has the world's largest collection of Confederate artifacts,

The Dictator lobbed 200-pound explosive shells more than two miles into Petersburg during the Union siege. The national battlefield park displays a replica of this impressive weapon.

Waiting was as difficult for Civil War soldiers in the trenches as it was for men in other wars. The exposed position of the officers indicates a lull in the fighting. Such opportunities did not occur often at Petersburg, where this picture was taken.

including the field uniforms of Lee, Jackson, Johnston, and Major General J.E.B. Stuart. Monument Avenue is so named because of its impressive monuments to Confederate heroes Lee, Jackson, Stuart, Davis, and the Virginian who became known as the "Pathfinder of the Seas," Matthew Fontaine Maury. In Hollywood Cemetery, along with two United States presidents and Confederate President Davis, lie the remains of 15,000 Confederate dead.

Lee evacuated Petersburg at night to gain time, a ruse that Union forces did not discover until 3 A.M. Grant then occupied Petersburg without resistance, but the 10-month siege had cost him 42,000 casualties and prisoners. Confederate losses numbered 28,000 men, who could not be replaced.

Lee's retreat was southwesterly, with Amelia Courthouse designated as the assembly point, but his lack of supplies proved costly; the need to forage enabled General Philip H. Sheridan's cavalry to get between Lee and Danville, through which Davis passed on the way south, and forced Lee to choose Lynchburg as an alternative. Fear that Lee would escape and unite with the western Confederate army, then falling back through the Carolinas before Sherman's drive, gave Grant extra incentive.

Lee's retreat was marred by the kind of mistakes made by tired officers overwhelmed by the problems confronting them, a combination of events that caused the normally imperturable Lee to question aloud whether his army was "disintegrating". Sayler's Creek Battlefield Historical State Park, off State Highway 307 and U.S. Route 306 a few miles east of Appomattox, commemorates the last full-scale battle fought by the Army of Northern Virginia, a battle that occurred only because Lee's rearguard mistakenly followed the wagon train along another route, and the rain-swollen creek delayed passage of the Confederate main body. The site, overlooking the small stream where Ewell's

Monument Avenue in Richmond is named for its equestrian statues of Virginia's heroes, including this one of General Lee.

St. Paul's Episcopal Church preserves many memories of the period when Richmond was the Confederate capital. Jefferson Davis was worshipping here when he received word to evacuate Richmond.

Corps successfully drove back the Union center but became surrounded, has paintings, maps, and recordings that explain the tragic battle that resulted in the surrender of 7,000 Confederate soldiers. Hillsman House, a white frame building on the hilltop from which Union forces attacked, dates from the 1770s and is restored outside to its appearance at the time of the Civil War.

In an engagement not far away, Major General John B. Gordon lost most of the Confederate wagon train and two-thirds of Lee's cannon but was able to avoid capture of his troops.

The loss of such quantities of men and supplies, along with the straggling and desertions resulting from a disjointed retreat, put Lee in an untenable position; but he still hoped his ragged and hungry

Libby Prison in Richmond consisted of several converted commercial structures commandeered to hold the large number of Union prisoners captured at First Manassas.

The White House of the Confederacy, a mansion originally built in 1817, was the residence of the Confederate president in Richmond; this view was taken around 1865. It is now part of the Museum of the Confederacy.

soldiers could break through Grant's tightening ring and unite with the Army of Tennessee under Johnston. The combined force could strike first one and then the other of the Union armies and gain more time for the Confederacy. Lee's last chance dissipated when General Gordon's attempt to create an escape route west of Appomattox could not be sustained without reinforcements — a situation that made the loss of 7,000 men at Sayler's Creek critical.

Lee considered courting death by leading a breakout charge, but this appealing alternative to surrender was overcome by his highly developed sense of duty. The South would need the leaders that remained to rebuild after four years of destructive warfare; the South could not afford to sacrifice brave men to futile

Jefferson Davis (left) was the first and only president of the Confederate States of America.

gestures. Lee swallowed his pride and agreed to meet with Grant to discuss surrender terms.

Appomattox Court House National Historical Park recreates the scene of the surrender. Lee and Grant met in the McLean House, which by an ironic twist of fate was owned by a farmer who had resettled there after his home at Manassas had been endangered by warfare. The present house is a reconstruction on the

The McLean House at Appomattox, where Lee surrendered the Army of Northern Virginia on Palm Sunday, 1865; this photo was taken shortly after that historic day. The house was dismantled for display after the war; it has been reconstructed on the original foundations and is authentically furnished.

From the porch of Kelly House, the occupants may have watched the tired Confederate veterans march by to surrender their weapons and flags. It now fronts on Surrender Triangle, where the story of the capitulation is told.

original foundations and is authentically restored inside. (The original was taken apart after the war, exhibited, and then stored at the Smithsonian Institution, where it deteriorated.) The replica of the room where the signing of the surrender took place on Palm Sunday 1865 is so expertly arranged one can almost see the two generals, flanked by aides, sitting at the tables across the room from each other.

Lee's intent was to get the best terms possible and to prevent his Army of Northern Virginia from being marched into captivity. Grant, still haunted by the fear that Lee might somehow escape, was generous: Lee's men were paroled to return to their homes, and the officers kept their sidearms to help preserve law and order; Grant also provided 25,000 rations for Lee's starving men. Lee and Grant would honor both the letter and the spirit of the agreement; Lee would never permit an unkind word about Grant in his presence, and Grant would threaten to resign his command if Lee were arrested and tried for treason. Lee also defended Grant's military record against postwar

detractors: "I have carefully searched the military records of both ancient and modern history, and have never found Grant's superior as a general," he said.

The paths at Appomattox Court House National Park lead through a village that looks much as it did in 1865. The reconstructed courthouse, which houses the Visitors' Center, museum, and slide show about the surrender, is the centerpiece of the restored village. Clustered around it are more than a dozen structures, including Clover Hill Tavern, the oldest surviving structure; Meek's Store and Woodson law office; and the Kelly and Isbel houses, which depict two quite different lifestyles of the period. The Old Richmond–Lynchburg Stage Road, along which the Union forces lined up to receive the Confederate surrender, leads past an area known as Surrender Triangle, where static displays and a recorded explanation recreate the surrender scene.

It was an electric moment when Confederate forces, led by General John B. Gordon, a capable and loyal Georgian, marched up the hill and along the road

This full-length portrait (right) of Robert E. Lee was taken by Matthew Brady shortly after the end of the war. Lee posed reluctantly, concerned that it might violate his parole.

The Court House hosts the Visitors' Center and museum at Appomattox National Historical Park, a recreation of the Civil War community.

bordered by Union troops. The Union line was called to attention in salute to the bravery of the men surrendering, and the Confederates returned the salute. There was little public display of exultation or rancor as the Southerners stacked arms and laid down their banners. Confederates who had existed for days on handfuls of parched corn wept and broke ranks to kiss the flags they were surrendering, but they obeyed Lee's eloquent surrender order, General Order No. 9, which put into words the thoughts of many of them: "I need not tell the brave survivors of so many hard fought battles, who have remained steadfast to the last, that I have consented to this result from no distrust of them; but feeling that valor and devotion could accomplish nothing that could compensate for the loss that must have attended the continuance of the contest, I determined to avoid the useless sacrifice of those whose past services have endeared them to their countrymen."

Men on both sides were relieved the bloodshed was over. Grant was already in Washington receiving the adulation of its citizens when Lee mounted Traveller and, with a few aides, rode to Richmond to rejoin his family as a private citizen. The cause of restoration that prevented his final defiant charge at Appomattox occupied the five years that remained to him. He accepted the presidency of tiny Washington College only after ascertaining that his association with the college would harm neither the institution nor its students; after his death it was renamed Washington and Lee University in his honor.

VIRGINIA
Stonewall's Valley

Winchester is especially beautiful in late spring, when the surrounding apple orchards are in bloom, valley wildlife is brilliant, and the distant hills are a hazy green. The "Gateway to the Shenandoah Valley" bustles then more than at any other time of the year as preparations are made for the annual Apple Blossom Festival and the arrival of a new influx of tourists along Interstate 81 and U.S. Route 11, which roughly follow the historic Valley Pike. During the Civil War, the influx was much more deadly. Winchester was the scene of more fighting than any other place in Virginia save Richmond. While war visited other places occasionally, it arrived in Winchester every year with the robins. The town changed hands more than 75 times, four of them in one fateful day. Only a shell of the neat, prosperous market community remained at the end of the war.

The four battles that took place there in 1862, 1863, and 1864 left 4,491 Union soldiers in the national cemetery, 2,381 of them unknown, and 3,829 Confederates in the Stonewall Cemetery, which is part of Mount Hebron Cemetery. Brigadier General Turner Ashby, Jackson's irrepressible cavalry chief who died in 1862 in a battle at Harrisonburg, is one of them.

The headquarters of Thomas Jonathan "Stonewall" Jackson, a handsome brick structure atop a knoll on North Braddock Street, holds a museum dedicated to the Confederate chieftain. Some of his personal effects are on display, along with other Civil War memorabilia. Major General Philip H. Sheridan used another house on Braddock Street as his headquarters during 1864, when he directed the campaign to so devastate the Valley that a crow flying over would have to carry its own provisions. His headquarters, now occupied by the Elks Club, is not open to the public.

The bronze Confederate Monument in front of the courthouse was erected in 1916.

Few traces of the four battlegrounds remain, but historical markers on Route 11 on the southern and northern sides of Winchester and at Kernstown identify the sites. Three miles from Winchester, on the north side of U.S. Route 522, are weathered earthworks raised by Federals when they occupied the town.

The Shenandoah Valley is "Stonewall's Valley". No other general is so closely identified with it, and not even Robert E. Lee rivaled Jackson for the affection of the inhabitants of this region. People sent letters to Confederate Secretary of War Judah P. Benjamin demanding that only Jackson defend the Valley, and then filled the ranks of the Stonewall Brigade with their sons. Mennonites who refused to fight sent wagons with supplies to his army. Citizens of towns frequently occupied by Federals turned out on their porches to wave and cheer whenever the Confederates came back. Jackson lived up to their trust in him. His 1862 Valley Campaign "whupped" an opponent three times his size so badly that Union armies were wary of Valley defenders long after Jackson's death in 1863.

Jackson possessed an odd sort of charisma. He was dour and aloof, a quiet man whose life centered on his family and his Presbyterian religious belief. He was a gentle, affectionate father to his family. His piety pervaded everything he did; he once said that "every thought should be a prayer." He shared Lee's belief that duty was a calling, not an elective. A graduate of West Point, Jackson was a professor at the Virginia Military Institute in Lexington, Virginia, when the war started. He volunteered immediately for active duty.

His first command, at Harper's Ferry, was a ragtag group of undisciplined recent civilians, known as the Army of the Shenandoah, who at first resented his harsh discipline and his dedication to year-round warfare. Jackson stayed close to his men and suffered along with them, so that soldiers waking with snow on their blankets in the mountains of West Virginia might see their commander rise from the ground a few feet from them. If they grumbled about their condition, and Jackson heard it, he did not remonstrate. Yet neither did he relent: Soldiers were supposed to endure hardships. They soon learned that combat and comfort did not coexist in Jackson's army and, while many thought him peculiar, they quickly came to trust and respect him. Jackson reciprocated by regarding no task beyond them.

This group, the 1st Virginia, became the Stonewall Brigade, which fought with great distinction from First Manassas to Appomattox. The men cheered when Jackson rode past them, even on secret marches, and loved him like a father even after his death. Strangely, Jackson's most famous nickname never appealed to his troops. He was "Old Jack" to most of them, and sometimes even "Old Blue Light" or "Hickory" — even "Square Box" because of his large shoe size — but men of the 1st Brigade seldom called him "Stonewall".

After First Manassas, where he acquired the nickname that helped make him a legend in his own time, Jackson was ordered to take command of Confederate forces in the Shenandoah Valley, which were part of the Army of Northern Virginia but operated independently most of the time. He was reluctant to leave the Stonewall Brigade, and a farewell address made at the request of his men told something about both of them. Rising in his stirrups before the massed brigade, he shouted: "In the Army of the Shenandoah you were the First Brigade! In the Army of the Potomac you were the First Brigade! In the Second Corps of the Army you are the First Brigade! You are the First Brigade in the affection of your general, and I hope by your future deeds and bearing you will be handed down as the First Brigade in this our Second War of Independence. Farewell!"

Colonel John S. Mosby's Rangers were one of the most feared cavalry units in the war. The irrepressible "Gray Ghost" is buried at Warrenton, Virginia.

Jackson's task in the Valley of Virginia was formidable. When he arrived at Winchester, he had only a force of militia to confront 27,000 Union troops spread out in western Virginia and another 18,000 camped on the north bank of the Potomac River. His separation from his brigade was brief, for it was soon sent to reinforce him, bringing the size of his force to 4,000 men.

Jackson's tactics for defense of the Valley were so masterful they were studied, along with some others from the American Civil War, in the military academies of Europe for many generations. Well into the twentieth century, military scholars debated the campaigns in print in Great Britain, France, and Germany. Field Marshal Erwin Rommel of Germany, who would later win fame in World War II as the "Desert Fox", was among those who visited the Shenandoah Valley in the 1930s to study the subject at first hand. Jackson's interest in holding the western counties of Virginia, which would break away from the South later in the war and form the state of West Virginia, showed a sense of strategy as well as well as tactics. He could see those valleys pointing straight at the cities of Pittsburgh, Harrisburg, and Philadelphia in Pennsylvania.

Professional military interest in Jackson's 1862 Valley campaign centers primarily on his achievements in mobility and deception. He moved infantry so fast his troops became known as "foot cavalry". His men were lean and lightly equipped; when Jackson had them leave their packs behind, they knew he meant business. (One historian believes his troops carried nothing but essentials and even preferred to carry their rations in their stomachs.) Jackson was relentless in pursuing an objective, and he personally prodded malingerers; the sight of Jackson inspired both hope and dread in tired, hungry men, but sometimes even this personal bond would not have sufficed. Jackson's edge was that both he and his men knew the terrain — every wind gap, every creek. They had played and hunted on the

hillsides and they had farmed the lowlands. They had excellent intelligence because they were among friends and neighbors who responded truthfully to the questions they asked. Furthermore, they knew how to use their advantage: On more than one occasion, Jackson moved his men away from his objective only to turn up like magic before a surprised foe.

Jackson employed all his knowledge and wits in the 1862 Valley campaign. He had 16,000 soldiers to counter three Union armies with a total of 65,000 men. His greatest danger was that those armies would unite against him, and his movements were designed to keep that from happening. He moved even before Brigadier General Richard S. Ewell's division arrived from east of the mountains to reinforce him. To deceive the Federals, Jackson marched his units eastward through the Blue Ridge Mountains to Mechum's River Station, where he put them on trains back to Staunton. He then moved northward along the Valley Pike, but veered westward to McDowell, where he routed two Union divisions. This battlefield is largely intact but is on private property, and so it is not developed for visitors.

"Old Jack" resumed his march up the Valley Pike to New Market, then turned eastward and disappeared into the small valley between the Massanutten and Blue Ridge mountains. After a forced march, including 26 miles in one 16-hour day, he fell upon the Union forces at Front Royal, threatening to trap Major General Nathaniel P. Banks in the Valley. A historical marker at the intersection of Royal Avenue and Chester Street in Front Royal and the Warren Rifles Confederate Museum recount the battle, including the mad dash to Winchester in which Jackson's men marched all night and went into battle with only an hour's rest. When they turned the Union right the line began to crumble, despite Banks's personal attempt to rally his men. The Union withdrawal soon turned into a Manassas-style rout,

*Union and Confederate
forces meet each year in a
re-enactment of the Battle
of New Market, complete
with smoke-filled
battlefields, produced by
firing cannons loaded with
blanks.*

*Signal towers, such as this
one at New Market,
Virginia, were in use
throughout the war.
Confederates used them to
signal with flags at First
Manassas.*

but the exhausted Confederates could not pursue adequately. They advanced all the way to Harper's Ferry, impeded only by a brief skirmish at Charlestown.

Prospect Hill Cemetery in Front Royal has two monuments, one of which recognizes the graves of 276 Confederate dead. The Mosby Monument commemorates seven of Mosby's Rangers who were executed illegally as spies by the Federals in the autumn of 1864.

Rebel control of the northern Shenandoah was brief: Jackson, now reinforced by Ewell and his men, had to pull back to meet a new threat from Major General John C. Frémont, with 16,000 troops, and Brigadier General James Shields, who was moving down from Manassas with 10,000. Encounters at Cross Keys and at Port Royal were two parts of a single battle. The first phase, at Cross Keys, saw a furious counterattack by Ewell's troops punishing Frémont. That success emboldened Jackson, who decided to hold off Frémont and attack Shields at Port Royal, then turn and deliver a decisive blow to Frémont. When the day was over, the Federals were in flight and the Valley was once again in Confederate hands. Jackson's loss was the greatest of his five-week campaign — 800 men.

On June 17, 1862, Jackson's army answered a call to help defend Richmond against McClellan's Peninsula campaign.

The Shenandoah Valley's best preserved battlefield, and the one most informative for the visitor, is not directly associated with Jackson. The Confederate general had been dead for a year when Federal forces approached New Market in a new attempt to occupy the narrow valley and thus simultaneously eliminate Virginia's breadbasket and flank Richmond. Nevertheless, one of the slide presentations at the New Market Battlefield Park is entitled "Stonewall's Valley" and relates his exploits. The Hall of Valor at New Market is more than a Civil War memorial; it honors the valor of American youth in all wars in defense of their country. Its

exhibits, however, place the New Market battle in the context of the larger Civil War struggle. A 28-foot-wide stained-glass window by Ami Shamir, an Israeli artist, incorporates the names of the Virginia Military Institute cadets killed at New Market and sets the mood for exhibits ranging from maps and photographs to a Napoleon 12-pounder cannon manned by mannequins.

The real story of New Market comes alive on the battlefield on the Sunday nearest the May 15 anniversary, when re-formed Civil War units reenact the battle. The view from the Bushong House up the slope where the boy soldiers from V.M.I. charged to capture several Federal cannon also provides an appreciation of their feat. The upperclassmen already had gone off to war when the call came. The younger cadets, in their early or middle teens, marched all night in the rain from Lexington to reach the scene. Intended as a reserve, they were mistakenly put into the assaulting line to the taunts and jeers of battle-hardened veterans flanking them. After the battle, the surviving cadets came back down the hill to the cheers of those who had taunted them before.

Few communities in the Confederacy contributed more to The Cause than Lexington, then a town of 2,500 inhabitants.

Lexington fielded both an artillery battery and an infantry company, and continued to send men to them throughout the war. On June 10, 1864, Union troops set fire to a considerable portion of the town, including V.M.I.

No community in the Shenandoah can match Lexington for its historical attractions. Robert E. Lee is buried there, in the Lee Chapel on the campus of Washington and Lee University. Lee was called to the presidency of the then-Washington College after the war and served the final five years of his life helping to educate the youth who would rebuild the South. Over his burial place is Edward Valentine's famous Recumbent Statue, which depicts Lee as commander of the Army of Northern Virginia resting on the battlefield. V.M.I. cadets, who today come from many states both North and South, salute as they pass the chapel.

Stonewall Jackson is buried in Lexington Cemetery, his grave topped by a tall memorial. When the column was dedicated in July 1891, aged and infirm survivors of the Stonewall Brigade disdained the comfort of homes in Lexington to bivouac "once more with Old Jack." Jackson's presence is felt elsewhere in Lexington. On East Washington Street stands the only home he ever owned, now a museum displaying relics of his life. A statue of Jackson, his face to the wind, faces the V.M.I. parade ground, not far from the Rockbridge Artillery Monument and a statue of Virginia Mourning Her Dead, which commemorates the cadets who fell at New Market.

At V.M.I., memory of New Market is more than a cold statue. Each May, the cadet corps forms in ranks on the drill field for a special roll call. As the names of the cadets who died at New Market are called off, someone in the ranks responds: "Died on the field of honor, Sir."

Armies passed through and camped near Strasburg many times, and fought for Fisher's Hill and Hupps Hill on U.S. Route 11 on both sides of town. A circle tour denotes the scene of the former, while remains of Federal trenches can be seen at the latter. North of Mt. Jackson, another often-visited place, an obelisk identifies the graves of 112 unknown Confederate soldiers. Edinburg was the scene of 28 skirmishes but is best known as the place where Sheridan, after setting fire to the grain mill, heeded the tearful pleas of two young ladies that the mill was the community's only means of livelihood and ordered that the flames be put out. The mill still stands.

The only house "Stonewall" Jackson ever owned (left) is now a shrine to his memory in Lexington, Virginia, where he taught and where he is buried.

(Facing Page:) At ceremonies each year, the Cadet Corps at Virginia Military Institute, shown in this aerial photo, memorializes "Stonewall" Jackson, a professor there at the start of the Civil War, and the boy soldiers of New Market.

Edward Valentine's Recumbent Statue of Lee (left) depicts the Confederate commander at rest on the battlefield. The statue is located over the Lee family crypt on the campus of Washington and Lee University.

Skirmishes occurred as far south as Salt-ville in southwest Virginia, an important source of salt for the Confederacy. It was seized by Union forces in 1864, and the salt works were destroyed.

The final battle for the Shenandoah was fought at Waynesboro on March 2, 1865, but the fate of the Valley had been determined the previous fall. The last major battle for the Valley was fought on October 19, 1864, at Cedar Creek on Belle Grove Plantation, one mile south of Middletown off U.S. Route 11. Confederate Lieutenant General Jubal A. Early caught Sheridan's men by surprise and had two Federal corps on the verge of rout until starving and ragged Confederate soldiers broke ranks to forage in the abandoned Federal camps. They were in no condition to resist Sheridan's counterattack. The Union general, 20 miles away when the battle began, added to his laurels and those of his horse, Rienzi, by riding hard and arriving at Cedar Creek in time to help rally his men. Rienzi, renamed Winchester after this ride, was eventually stuffed and given to the Smithsonian Instiuation, where he can still be seen.

The battlefield is intact but undeveloped, except for historical markers. Belle Grove, the 1794 mansion that Sheridan used as headquarters, it now a museum.

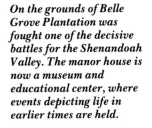

On the grounds of Belle Grove Plantation was fought one of the decisive battles for the Shenandoah Valley. The manor house is now a museum and educational center, where events depicting life in earlier times are held.

WEST
VIRGINIA
Political Prize

T he western counties of Virginia were more a political prize than a strategic plum during the War Between the States. While the earliest fighting of the war occurred there — Philippi is said to be the first major battlefield — the 26 sparsely settled counties were spared because of their difficult terrain, isolation, and poverty from becoming a major scene of battle. West Virginia was even more divided by the war than western Maryland was, Stonewall Jackson had been born at Clarksburg and raised at Jackson Mill near Weston, and many mountain men followed him into Confederate gray. The Confederate spies Belle Boyd and Nancy Hart were western Virginians. But these counties had always been suspicious of the lowlands, which controlled the government far away in Richmond. The inhabitants were small farmers and miners, for the most part, who owned few slaves and whose loyalty was to themselves more than to any cause or any government.

Virginia tried at first to hold onto the area. Jackson, in particular, thought the valleys along the forks of the Potomac had strategic value and he occupied Romney in his first campaign. Even the dead of winter could not keep Jackson idle. Reinforced by 7,000 men under Brigadier General W.W. Loring, he moved against Romney, 35 miles from Winchester, which was defended by Brigadier General B.F. Kelley with 5,000 men in blue. Jackson's move was hampered by the softness of his troops, a lack of equipment, and the reluctance of Loring, but Stonewall managed to destroy the Baltimore & Ohio Railway bridge over the Great Cacapon River and to occupy Romney, which Kelley evacuated. Jackson left Loring to hold Romney and returned to Winchester with the Stonewall Brigade. Loring's fears that he would be cut off, fed by grumbling of the officers at

Romney, led Confederate Secretary of War Judah P. Benjamin to tell Jackson "to order him [Loring] back immediately." Jackson dutifully obeyed orders but submitted his request to resign or to be returned to teaching duty at the Virginia Military Institute. Neither was accepted, but Benjamin got the message and thereafter was less eager to inject politics into military affairs.

A Confederacy short on manpower, as well as everything else, could not spare the means to hold western Virginia against a Federal army that numbered more than 27,000, at times. Federal interest was political, and in June 1861 West Virginians were induced to hold a constitutional convention in Wheeling and secede from Virginia. In June 1863, the United States Congress voted West Virginia into the Union as a separate state. Thus there were

John Brown (right), the fiery abolitionist from Kansas, led a raid on the arsenal at Harper's Ferry, West Virginia, in 1859. It resulted in his execution and martyrdom in the antislavery cause.

Harper's Ferry, taken and retaken several times during the Civil War, looks much the same today (right) as it did in 1865, when the picture above was taken. The community now is a national historic site explaining the development of weapons and its varied history as an arsenal.

West Virginians fighting on both sides for most of the war, as the Confederate monument in Union, West Virginia, shows.

The mountainous terrain in West Virginia restricted maneuvering by large units, and this kept the battles relatively small. Harper's Ferry, the object of John Brown's famous raid on the Federal arsenal in 1859, witnessed the most substantial fighting. It was taken by the Confederates on several occasions, only to be abandoned to the Federals because the surrounding hills, looking down on the town, made it almost indefensible. Its principal buildings, including the armory, arsenal, and mills, were destroyed during the war.

Harper's Ferry National Historical Park depicts a mid–nineteenth-century community as well as a Civil War battlefield. The Master Armorer's House, a museum of the history of gunmaking, which has a collection of weapons, and the late–eighteenth-century Harper House, the oldest surviving structure, are the leading display buildings. Others include the blacksmith shop, drug store, tavern, and armorer's house. Park rangers conduct tours and give living-history demonstrations in the streets. The Stone Steps, hand carved in the living rock, lead to a view of the Potomac and Shenandoah river valleys that Thomas Jefferson described in 1783 as "stupendous". The viewpoint is called Jefferson Rock.

Areas outside Harper's Ferry that are included in this national park include Bolivar and Loudoun Heights in West Virginia, Maryland Heights in Maryland, and Short Hill in Virginia. Jackson's successful attack against Union defenders in 1862 started on Bolivar Heights. A walking trail visits the remains of some of the Union breastworks.

The first fighting in West Virginia occurred when Union forces engaged Confederate artillery at Seawell's Point, but the distinction of having the first battle goes to Philippi. A splendid old covered bridge still standing over the Tygart River was used by both armies; there are histor-ical markers. The Battle of Philippi, on June 3, 1861, was an easy Union victory, as Union forces under then-Colonel Kelley surprised newly recruited Confederates under Colonel G.A. Porterfield and sent them scurrying. The "Philippi races" helped pro-Unionists maintain control of

This old covered bridge at Philippi, West Virginia, accommodated the crossing of armies from both sides during the war, but the nearby battle was a Union victory that helped pro-Unionists retain control of the state.

West Virginia and may have given General Irvin McDowell's army, gathering near Manassas for the drive on Richmond, a feeling of overconfidence.

The Gauley Bridge over the New River was the scene of heavy fighting in 1861, when Federal troops under Brigadier General William S. Rosecrans defeated the Confederates, who destroyed the bridge to protect their retreat. Only the damaged piers remain, upstream from the new bridge.

Another significant battle, on September 10, 1861, is remembered at Carnifex Ferry Battlefield, near Summerfield on State Route 39. The Patteson House, trapped between the lines of the two armies, has been restored and houses a museum with Civil War relics. Summerfield itself became a battlefield and was burned when Nancy Hart, a Confederate spy, led an attack that captured the Union force there.

The largest Civil War engagement in West Virginia took place on a high plateau at Droop Mountain on November 6, 1863. Defeat in the fierce fighting ended Southern efforts to hold the state. Part of the battlefield has been restored and marked for visitors, and a small museum displays Civil War relics; the site is along U.S. Route 219. Hiking trails explore the forests and overlook the Greenbrier Valley.

Confederate units marched through Martinsburg, the home of spy Belle Boyd, on both invasions of the North. Fighting occurred at Lewisburg, in the southeastern part of the state, on May 22, 1862, and resulted in a Union victory. Soldiers killed in the battle are buried in a mass grave at the intersection of U.S. 60 and McElhenny Road. Other fighting took place at Rich Mountain near Beverly and at Laurel Hill.

West Virginia, which defected from Virginia, pays great homage to a famous son who didn't. A statue of Thomas J. "Stonewall" Jackson stands near the blue-and-gold dome of the West Virginia state Capitol in Charleston.

Nancy Hart of West Virginia spied for the Confederacy and led a raid against Union forces camped at Summerfield.

Belle Boyd was only a teenager when she began to hate the Union troops occupying West Virginia. In time, she became one of the Confederacy's greatest spies.

MARYLAND
The War Goes North

I t was a strange sight. Tough, battle-hardened veterans, lean from hunger and wearing tattered uniforms, sang "Maryland, My Maryland" like recruits on the drill field as they stretched out for miles along dusty roads. There was good reason for their high spirits and the spring in their step; they were carrying the war to the North for the first time.

Maryland was bitterly divided by the Civil War. Although the state remained in the Union, the decision was made as much by geography as by sentiment. At the oubreak of war, Union troops marching to the defense of Washington were stoned by civilians in Baltimore, which would remain a hotbed of secessionist sentiment throughout the conflict. Maryland units fought on both sides; but in general eastern Maryland was more sympathetic to the Southern cause than western Maryland, which was populated by farmers who were proud of the accomplishments of their own hands and who owned few slaves. Most just wanted both armies to leave them alone to work their fields.

That was not to be. Invasion of the Confederate states by Union forces produced a sharp public reaction and a demand for retaliation. The idea of invasion had logistic and strategic appeal for the Confederacy, too. An invasion of the North would enable the Southern army to draw supplies from what Lieutenant General James Longstreet called the "bounteous land" of Maryland without further impoverishing areas of Virginia already well worked over, would "bring the war home" to Northerners, who so far had suffered few ill effects, and would soothe Southern feelings wounded by the deprivations of war. Success might produce good results abroad, too, in the form of recognition by one or more of the major European powers — and that would perhaps enable

General George B. McClellan commanded the Northern army at the Battle of Antietam. Although he stopped Lee's invasion of Maryland, he was later dismissed by Lincoln because of his bad case of the "slows."

This sunken country road is clearly visible from a postwar memorial tower, but it was hidden from the view of participants in the Battle of Antietam. It was known as Bloody Lane by the time the fighting ended. Confederates and Federals fought a four-hour, see-saw battle to possess this strategic point.

the South to break the blockade that was causing cotton and tobacco to pile up in warehouses and hindering the importation of badly needed munitions. General Robert E. Lee further saw it as an opportunity for Confederate President Jefferson Davis to make a proposal for peace, which, "being made when it is in our power to inflict injury upon our adversary, would show conclusively to the world that our sole object is the establishment of our independence and the attainment of an honorable peace."

Lee's victory at the second battle of Manassas (Bull Run) provided the opportunity and the means to carry the war to the North. He moved cautiously across the Potomac near Leesburg, with J.E.B. Stuart's cavalry between his army and Washington. He planned to protect his other flank by clearing the Federal troops from Harper's Ferry and then bringing his army together to continue the invasion, perhaps into Pennsylvania.

Things did not go as well as he hoped. On September 13, 1862, while General Thomas J. "Stonewall" Jackson was converging on Harper's Ferry, a lost copy of Lee's battle order was found by a Union private and reached General George McClellan in plenty of time to strike Lee

while his army was divided. McClellan's affliction with the "slows" enabled Lee, who learned from a Southern sympathizer that McClellan was in possession of the order, to move reinforcements to guard the passes of South Mountain. McClellan attacked the passes on September 14, and for a time Lee considered withdrawing from Maryland without further contest. He changed his mind when he received word that Jackson had captured Harper's Ferry, taken 11,000 Federal prisoners, and would soon be on his way to join Lee.

By then, Lee's army was concentrated on high ground west of Antietam Creek and across the angle formed by the junction of the creek with the Potomac River. Why Lee chose to fight there is a mystery. It was a tactically strong position, except that the streams blocked the avenue of retreat, but it was not a good one from which to continue an advance northward. Jackson's arrival on the eve of the September 17, 1862, battle brought Lee's strength to 40,000, far too few to press the invasion as long as McClellan's 87,000 blocked the way.

Antietam is one of the most beautiful of the Civil War battlefields. The view from the entrance to the Visitors' Center on Maryland Route 65 looks back across rolling fields toward Sharpsburg; in the other direction lie more undulating fields, sometimes interrupted by those sharp breaks that created problems for Union attackers and produced such colorful names as Bloody Lane. The terrain preserved in Antietam National Battlefield Park makes it easy to understand why the Union attack was not as coordinated as McClellan wished. But it is so beautiful and peaceful today that the visitor has difficulty realizing that this was the scene of the bloodiest single day of the Civil War. As night fell on September 17, 1862, these fields were strewn with dead bodies and wounded men crying for help, pockmarked with shell holes, and littered with smashed equipment. The carnage was "too fearful to contemplate" even for battle-wise General James Longstreet. Federal losses at Antietam came to 12,410 and Confederate losses were only slightly less at 10,700.

The remains of 4,776 Union soldiers are buried in Antietam National Cemetery on State Route 34 at its entrance to Sharpsburg, a high point with a gothic chapel overlooking part of the battlefield. The dead are buried in surrounding communities, as well. Most of the Confederates are buried in Hagerstown and Frederick, where Barbara Fritchie had defiantly flown the Stars and Stripes as Confederate troops marched past, and in Shepardstown, West Virginia. The Fritchie House preserves the memory and a few relics of the 96-year-old woman whose act made her a folk heroine and immortalized her in a ballad by famed poet John Greenleaf Whittier.

Cannon between the Visitors' Center and the restored Dunker Church stand on the spot from which Confederate artillery swept the Cornfield and the East Woods as Federals attacks. Photographs taken after the battle show clusters of dead Confederate gunners lying around some of their cannon. On the nearby hilltop stands one of many monuments in the park, this one erected by the State of New York to commemorate its sons who took part in the momentous struggle. Cannon situated in appropriate places in the park help tell the story of the furious cannonading during the battle, which some historians describe as principally an artillery duel. During the warm months, as part of the living-history presentation, park rangers show all the steps needed to fire the Parrotts and the six- and ten-pounders. Other interpretive programs depict camp life, calvalry drills, the role of women in the war, and the history of the Dunker Church.

More than any other battlefield, Antietam demonstrates the important role women played throughout the war in dealing with the fighting's aftermath on the battlefield. Clara Barton was a Patent Office clerk who followed McClellan's

army from Washington to tend the wounded. She brought medical supplies and food from Washington during the early hours of the fighting, before the regular army supplies arrived. Afterward she saw men die at night because doctors did not have enough light to tend them, and too few doctors were available, anyway, to care for the thousands who fell during the day. Antietam made an indelible impression on Clara Barton. She convinced the chief quartermaster in Washington to provide wagons and supplies for a number of later battles and became superintendent of nurses of the Army of the James in 1864. In 1877, after further experience in Europe, she founded the American Red Cross on the concept of providing aid and comfort during disaster in both war and peace.

The dead littered the fields and woods near the Dunker Church after the Battle of Antietam. The reconstructed church is now one of the principal landmarks of the battlefield.

Monuments line Cornfield Avenue at Antietam, which cuts through the original field. The fighting was so heavy there that the cornstalks were cut down as though by scythes.

Two audio-visual presentations at the Visitors' Center depict the significant events of the battle and President Abraham Lincoln's visit immediately afterward. Lincoln inspected the battlefield, consoled the wounded, and questioned McClellan about his slow pursuit. The photograph of Lincoln and McClellan sitting and talking in the command tent is one of the most famous of the war; what was said is a mystery.

The eight-mile self-drive tour of the park covers the three phases of the battle in order, beginning with the dawn attack from Joseph Poffenberger's farm on Stonewall Jackson's men in the Cornfield. Attackers and defenders charged between head-high rows of cornstalks and the battle surged back and forth until, in the words of Union General Joseph Hooker, "every stalk of corn in the northern and greater part of the field was cut as closely as could have been done with a knife, and the slain lay in rows as precisely as they had stood in their ranks a few moments before." The fighting continued for three hours, and the field changed hands 14 times in the heaviest fighting of the day. Cornfield Avenue, lined with monuments and interpretive markers and paintings, leads through the area and to the East Woods, from which Union Major General John Sedgwick launched his division against Jackson's defensive line in the West Woods. It was the costliest action of the bloodiest day: In less than half an hour Sedgwick lost more than 2,200 men. The tall monument in the West Woods to the

Clara Barton, founder of the American Red Cross, began her crusade to save the lives of wounded Union soldiers at Antietam. Later, she was commissioned as superintendent of nurses and also served on other battlefields.

President Abraham Lincoln, who inspected the Antietam battlefield immediately after the battle in 1862, posed for this photo with McClellan and his generals.

2nd Philadephia Brigade does not convey adequately the high drama that occurred on this strategic spot.

An observation tower provides a good view of the rolling terrain of the battlefield. It overlooks the Sunken Road, the principal feature of the second phase of the battle. Fighting between Union and Confederate infantry in this area lasted four hours and caused so many casualties the road was nicknamed Bloody Lane. The fighting finally just petered out because of confusion and exhaustion.

The third phase of the battle reached a climax late in the afternoon at the Antietam Bridge, now named the Burnside Bridge after Ambrose Burnside, the Union general who commanded the assault against some four hundred well-

other end of the battlefield. At 1 P.M., Burnside finally forced a crossing and gradually pushed the Georgians back, but re-forming his lines for a frontal assault took two hours, during which Confederate reinforcements arrived.

Although the action in this area was minor compared to the carnage elsewhere, Burnside's crossing created a major threat to Lee's army. Control of Sharpsburg would cut Lee's line of retreat. The ability of Confederate leaders to move men to the right place at the right time saved the day. About 4 P.M., Major General A.P. Hill's division, which had remained in Harper's Ferry to dispose of captured Federal property and parole prisoners, arrived and immediately drove Burnside back to the heights near the bridge.

The timely arrival of forces under General A.P. Hill protected Lee's line of retreat from Sharpsburg.

A small Confederate force held off a major Union attack at Antietam Bridge, protecting Lee's flank while the battle raged elsewhere.

entrenched Georgia veterans guarding the crossing. A path leads down the hill from the Confederate defenses and across the bridge to. the area where Union men formed up to charge. The wooded ground around the bridge today is quite different from the open area that helped the sharpshooters keep Burnside's men from crossing for hours while the battle raged at the

The costly battle was over. The next day, Lee ended his first invasion of the North by withdrawing across the Potomac, none of his objectives fulfilled. The cautious McClellan licked his wounds and let him go, a decision that was to cost him command of the Army of the Potomac.

The Battle of Antietam gave Lincoln many of the things he desired. McClellan

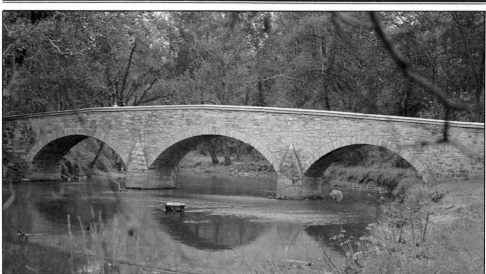

The contrast between the terrain at Antietam in 1862 and now is apparent. Antietam Bridge is now called the Burnside Bridge, after the Union general who captured it too late to affect the battle.

had pressed the attack once he was ready, and his ability to hold the field ended the myth of Lee's invincibility. It also halted the invasion of Maryland at the outset, and so was a blow to Confederate hopes for recognition by European powers. Thus, although the battle was tactically a draw, it was a strategic victory for the North and created an atmosphere that permitted Lincoln to issue the Emancipation Proclamation, which declared the slaves in the Confederate states to be free. The positive results of the battle were not enough to save McClellan, however; on November 5 Lincoln replaced him with Burnside.

Antietam was the only major battle fought in Maryland. Lee passed through western Maryland en route to the fateful battle at Gettysburg in neighboring Pennsylvania, and, almost to the end, sizable Confederate raids attempted to draw forces away from the siege of Richmond and Petersburg. Union burning and looting in the Shenandoah Valley, including the destruction of the Virginia Military Institute and the home of Governor Letcher, had not left the Confederates in a generous mood. They ripped up the tracks of the Baltimore & Ohio Railway, which already had suffered considerably, extacted tribute from the town of Frederick, and seized horses, cattle, and forage.

In July 1864, General Jubal A. Early led his troops against Washington, whose strong fortifications had been stripped of manpower to replace Grant's heavy losses. Grant detached the veteran 6th Corps and sent it by water to reinforce the undermanned fortifications, and thus Early's brisk jabs at Fort Stevens accomplished little but to scare Washington residents and create an opportunity for an American president in office to see a battle. Lincoln arrived during fighting outside Fort Stevens and climbed the parapet to watch. He ignored pleas to take cover until Brigadier General Horatio Wright threatened to have his commander-in-chief forcibly removed. An amused Lincoln obeyed orders. Fort Stevens no longer exists, but the incident and the fighting are commemorated each year at Fort Ward in Alexandria, Virginia.

The prison camp at Point Lookout, where 20,000 Confederate soldiers were held, was a possible secondary objective for Early, but it was never reached. The beautiful sandy point where the Potomac River and Chesapeake Bay meet, now a state park, gives little indication of the Andersonville-like reputation the prisoner-of-war camp had. More than three thousand prisoners died there. They are buried in the national cemetery, where monuments erected by both the state and federal governments honor their memory.

PENNSYLVANIA
The Highwater Mark

Everything about the Gettysburg battlefield is grand. It is the largest contiguous battlefield park in the nation, the most commercialized, and the one that accommodates the most visitors. It is also the most developed, with more than 1,000 monuments and cannon along 40 miles of scenic roads, and has the most impressive monuments — all of which make it easy to follow and understand the decisive battle that took place there July 1–3, 1863.

The grandeur is justified. Gettysburg was a watershed in the Civil War. It halted the last invasion of the North by the South, and it ended for all time the hope that European powers would recognize the independence of the Confederacy. The war would last almost two years more and General Robert E. Lee would lead his Army of Northern Virginia to victory again, but the tide of the Confederacy began to ebb when even the bravery of Major General George E. Pickett's men could not break the Union center at the Angle and the Copse of Trees.

Yet Gettysburg became a battlefield more by chance than by design. On June 3, after his stunning victory at Chancellorsville against a vastly superior force, Lee marched north again in an attempt to take pressure off Vicksburg, then under siege. He passed through western Maryland and into Pennsylvania, with Harrisburg, its capital, as the objective. Union forces under General Joseph Hooker paralleled his route in order to protect Washington and Baltimore, but Hooker resigned as commander of the Army of the Potomac and was succeeded by General George Gordon Meade. Lee ordered his army, by then almost at the Susquehanna River, to turn back to Cashtown, and units of the two armies met by chance at Gettysburg on June 30. The next day the battle was joined as Confederates drove the

General George Gordon Meade was in command at Gettysburg. He was the fifth commander of the Union army in less than 12 months.

Federals through Gettysburg to a line formed by Culps Hill, Cemetery Ridge, and Little Round Top south of town. Lee moved his forces to Seminary Ridge, almost a mile from the Union line, placing them in a north-south arc that stretched almost five miles.

The fighting that started late on July 2 continued until 10 o'clock at night as Lee sought to turn the Union flanks before Meade could concentrate all his forces. General James Longstreet, who was to attack the critical left flank, would spend the remainder of his life denying that his delays cost the Confederacy a victory at Gettysburg; but it was not until 4 P.M. that his cannon roared into action preceding the attack. By then, fresh Union troops had moved into the Wheatfield and Devil's Den, names that by nightfall would become immortalized by the blood of thousands of dead and wounded soldiers. Nor was General Dick (Old Bald Head) Ewell's attack on the other flank an unmitigated success; it lacked coordination and bogged down as additional infantry units and cannon joined General Meade's line of blue. Delays had cost Lee a decisive victory.

The third day, July 3, was a classic example of infantry attack. Union regulars regained ground on their right flank, putting both flanks in almost impregnable positions. This forced Lee to make a frontal assault on the center of the line, where a breakthrough would divide the Union army and win the battle. Longstreet had objections, as he always did, but Lee was determined: "The enemy is there, and I am going to strike him," he said, pointing at Cemetery Ridge. What followed has gone down in history as a symbol of Southern courage, under the name Pickett's Charge.

Confederate General James Longstreet's delay in carrying out the order to attack at Gettysburg would haunt him the remainder of his life.

The yard of the Trostle Farmhouse is littered with dead animals after the Battle of Gettysburg. The 9th Massachusetts battery, which set up there, lost most of its horses.

Seen from either side of the battlefield, from the Angle and the Copse of Trees on Cemetery Ridge — at which the charge was aimed — or from the Virginia Monument near the Confederate center, the heroism of the charge is evident. Almost a mile of open field slopes gradually down from one ridge and up to the other. There is no protection, no place to pause. The 12,000-man gray wave, led by bright regimental flags, advanced at a walk most of the distance, their lines shredded by double cannister shells and sharp-shooting riflemen in the Union defenses. The Rebels charged at a run only the last quarter-

mile, into a barrier of smoke created by the deadly firing from the ridge ahead. It was a magnificent effort that almost worked. The Confederates breached the blue Union line near the Copse of Trees but were too few and too exhausted to hold the ground. As they drew back across the open field their casualties continued to mount, and when the 50 minutes of combat were over, 10,000 of them had fallen.

The next day was the Fourth of July, the birthday of the United States, and the battle did not resume. Lee's losses during the three days of battle, a staggering 28,000, represented nearly 38 percent of his 75,000-man army, and he could no longer press the fight. Meade, who had lost 23,000 of his 97,000 men, pursued, but the chase was rendered ineffective by Confederate rearguards and by rain. Lee's retreat was made even more bitter by "dispiriting news" that Vicksburg had fallen and the South was cut in two.

Gettysburg is the most visible American battlefield. It can be viewed in electric-map and static display form at the Visitors' Center, on a cyclorama housed in its own building, and from an observation tower. Airplanes carry visitors on regular flights over the 25 square miles of the battlefield. The most popular method of visitation remains the drive-through tour, which follows both the lines of the last two days of the battle and the major points of the initial day's combat.

The drive begins at the cyclorama and follows a road bearing the names (consecutively) of Union Generals Hancock, Sedgwick, Sykes, Warren, and Crawford and running among dozens of monuments, large and small. General Meade is memorialized by a large equestrian statue, while nearby a small monument recognizes the 1st Pennsylvania Cavalry. Pennsylvania and other states have raised impressive memorials along this part of the drive.

An artillery battery at the Angle (sometimes called the Bloody Angle) looks out over the ground covered by Pickett's Charge. A copse of trees stands nearby, as

Fields littered with bodies (left) were a trademark of the Gettysburg battle as Lee sent his troops against both flanks and the center of the Union line. Combined casualties for both sides totaled around 50,000.

A medical tent (left) serves as a field hospital for an emergency amputation at Gettysburg.

it did in 1863, and a tablet identifies the spot as the High Water Mark of the Confederacy. That was where Pickett's men stopped and, although they did not realize it at the time, the days of the Confederacy were numbered.

The drive crosses Little Round Top and skirts Big Round Top, where a one-hour circular walking trail winds through a typical Pennsylvania hardwood forest and passes a stone wall built for defense by Union troops. Then the driving tour meanders through terrain Federal units occupied on the second day while the Confederates dallied.

Memorials in the Wheatfield and Death Valley recall the terrible toll of the day's fighting, and a path leads onto the rocks called Devil's Den, from which sharpshooters poured deadly fire.

Confederate Avenue, along Lee's battle line, has fewer memorials and cannon, but the ones there are among the most expressive on the battlefield. Alabama mourns

A jumble of rocks known as Devil's Den at the foot of Little Round Top hid sharpshooters during the Battle of Gettysburg, but not always well enough. This young soldier was killed as Confederate General Hood's men were repulsed.

her fallen sons at Biesecker Woods. A feature of the Virginia Memorial, which stands on the spot near the center of the line from which Lee watched Pickett's Charge, is an equestrian statue of Lee on a high pedestal. Figures around the base of the statue represent the actions of various types of workers who left civilian life to become soldiers. The smaller, but equally impressive, North Carolina Memorial is to Lee's left, in the area where men of that state marshalled to join Pickett's Charge.

The park road also runs along McPherson and Oak ridges, where the battle began as a chance encounter, to the Etenal Light Peace Memorial, which was dedicated in 1938, on the 75th anniversary of the battle, to "Peace Eternal in a Nation Unified."

A short drive through Gettysburg reveals privately owned attractions ranging from the National Civil War Wax Museum to the Lincoln Train Museum. Life styles of the Civil War era are recreated during Heritage Days each July. The driving tour then reaches Culp's Hill and Spangler Spring, where seesaw fighting occurred on the second day of the battle.

Gettysburg National Cemetery, across the street from the entrance to the Visitors' Center, has 3,585 plain white headstones and a tall, lean Soldiers' Monument acknowledging their supreme sacrifice. In fact, the cemetery is better known for a speech that contains just 10 sentences. President Abraham Lincoln was not the principal speaker at the dedication of the national cemetery on November 19, 1863, and had been invited only as a formality. Edward Everett, considered one of the greatest orators of the time, spoke for almost two hours — and nobody today remembers what he said. Lincoln's address, which took only two minutes to deliver and was heard by few in the audience, not only is engraved on a memorial in the cemetery but also is world famous as an expression of hope that good can arise from the sacrifices of war.

An event incidental to the battle was the burning of Carlisle Cavalry Barracks north of Gettysburg. General J.E.B. Stuart's cavalry had moved into Pennsylvania independently, east of both Lee and Meade, and had been shadowed as far as Hanover by Union cavalry. Unable to find where the main Confederate force was, Stuart pushed on to Carlisle, where he hoped to obtain rations. When he learned that Union troops were lying in ambush in Carlisle homes, he sent a flag of truce with an offer: surrender or be bombarded.

Union soldiers who died at Gettysburg are commemorated by the Soldier's National Monument in the cemetery where President Lincoln delivered his famous Gettysburg Address.

The Pennsylvania Memorial stands near the center of the Union line on Cemetery Hill. This photo looks eastward along the ridge.

When the offer was refused he began shelling the town, then ordered his men to set fire to the United States cavalry barracks. These were rebuilt in 1864 and still form an active army post.

Chambersburg was burned in 1864 during a cavalry raid intended to retaliate for destruction of private property in Virginia. Two-thirds of the city was destroyed after it failed to pay an indemnity it was not likely to raise on short notice — $100,000 in gold or $500,000 in greenbacks. The action was not popular with the Confederates involved; in fact, Colonel William F. Peters of the 23rd Virginia Cavalry refused to obey the order to burn the town and was placed under temporary arrest.

Whereas death was ever present and destruction had become commonplace in a war that had intensified in bitterness, sanity had not been totally subordinated. The remaining two years of war would test it sorely, however, as the war moved deeper into the South.

NORTH CAROLINA

Surrender

They knew each other well — they had fought, sparred, and maneuvered across several states — but they did not meet until April 17, 1865, when they rode under flags of truce to a dusty crossroads in central North Carolina: Confederate General Joseph E. Johnston, commander of the largest Southern army remaining in the field, and Union Major General William Tecumseh Sherman, whose troops had scourged and pillaged the South from Atlanta to Savannah and then through the Carolinas. The site of their negotiations was the Bennett farmhouse. Now restored to about the way it looked at the time of the historic meeting, it is the centerpiece of the Bennett Place State Historical Park near Durham.

Behind closed doors, the generals talked for a long time about the political status of the Southern states that had seceded. Johnston had authority from Confederate President Jefferson Davis, and Sherman thought he was "fully empowered to arrange . . . any terms for the suspension of hostilities." Sherman was aware that President Abraham Lincoln had been assassinated, but had not announced it to either his troops or Johnston. The first meeting of the generals would last two days and produce an agreement that, in addition to disbanding of the Confederate army, specifically included a general amnesty "so far as the executive can command" and a guarantee of political, property, and personal rights "as defined in the Constitution of the United States and of the states respectively." This was too generous for the government in Washington, disturbed by the recent assassination of Lincoln. Washington would accept only the terms that General Ulysses S. Grant had given General Robert E. Lee at Appomattox. The chance to avoid the most bitter part of the War Between the States —

Reconstruction — was lost.

Johnston disobeyed orders from a disappointed Jefferson Davis and surrendered his forces, already badly depleted by walk-outs who had started home when the first agreement became known.

The Bennett farmhouse where the two momentous meetings occurred burned in 1921 but has been restored around the stone chimney, which survived the fire. The furnishings in the sitting room differ somewhat from those depicted in contemporary drawings made by artists not present at the talks, but the rooms and simple furniture are as authentic as possible. Two downstairs bedrooms are authentically furnished, too; one of them has a bed with rope in place of slatting.

A detached log-cabin kitchen, where Lucy Bennett and her children may have waited while the generals used her home, is dominated by a huge stone fireplace and equipment that includes pots and pans, buckets, a spinning wheel, pottery and porcelain, and a log kitchen table with chairs and one high-chair.

Exhibits in the Visitors' Center relate the Bennett Place surrender to the earlier surrender at Appomattox and include a copy of the surrender terms and of Johnston's order to his army to disband after "every hope of success by war" was gone. Photographs and displays illustrate the destruction the war had caused in the South.

On a slight mound in front of the farmhouse stands the Unity Monument. Its two columns, joined by a cap, are symbolic of the reuniting of the two parts of the country after the Civil War.

Although North Carolina was late in joining the Confederacy, and even had a rump group that tried to cancel secession, the state was a major source of supplies and manpower for the Confederacy throughout the Civil War. From its farms and factories and through its ports flowed the food and materials that kept the Army of Northern Virginia in the field, despite persistent complaints among the local population about a rich man's war and a poor man's fight. North Carolina, with one-ninth of the population of the Confederacy, provided almost one-sixth of the troops, most of them volunteers. Soldiers from North Carolina fought and died in every battle in the east and some in the west. The first Confederate to die, in the little-known Battle of Big Bethel in Hampton, Virginia, was Private Henry Lawson Wyatt, who is appropriately remembered

General Joseph E. Johnston commanded the Confederate army confronting General William T. Sherman as it marched northward from Savannah.

by a statue on the lawn of the Old Capitol Building in Raleigh. Approximately 40,000 from North Carolina — more than from any other Southern state — died in uniform. Almost one-fourth of the Confederate combat losses — 19,673 — were North Carolinians.

Home-front sacrifices were great, too. North Carolina officials and citizens sustained their own troops in Virginia and Tennessee and at the same time were faced with invasions at home from the east, west, and south — and marauders in the western mountains. Fighting, though on a smaller scale than in Virginia, Tennessee, and along the Mississippi River, was constant in the state.

The war came first to the coastal region, where four Federal installations — Forts Macon, Caswell, and Johnston and the Fayetteville Arsenal — had been taken over by North Carolinian state forces.

After President Lincoln declared a blockade of the Confederate coastline, Union efforts were aimed at closing the major ports. Fort Fisher, which controlled the entrance to the Cape Fear River and the port of Wilmington (N.C.) and often was described as "the Gibraltar of America", was considered too strong for the Union forces to take at that time. As a result, Union efforts were concentrated on controlling the Pamlico Sound, where there were a number of bay and river ports. Blockade runners using those ports had Hatteras Inlet as their major point of ingress and egress.

The series of attacks on North Carolina coastal targets brought into being the United States army's first major amphibious force and created a variety of landing techniques that would be perfected in later wars. The first amphibious operation of the Civil War captured Cape Hatteras, the strategic elbow island on the Outer Banks, now a prime vacation area but one whose offshore waters are still infamous for peculiar currents and violent storms. During a two-day battle, Forts Hatteras and Clark were reduced by gunfire from a fleet of eight warships. Then two troopships arrived, bringing soldiers from Fortress Monroe in Virginia to capture the forts and more than 600 Confederate prisoners. Loss of Hatteras was a blow to Confederate efforts to keep imports flowing because it deprived blockade runners of the most convenient entrance to Pamlico Sound.

Comments by Confederate prisoners after the battle indicated they placed too much confidence in newly invented water mines placed at Hatteras Inlet. It had been expected that these could damage the attacking Federal fleet. An article in *The Washington Star* belittled the inventor, Matthew F. Maury, as a "trickster" and Confederates as "credulous enough to put faith in his pretentions to the extent that by his wonderful submarine batteries and other kickshaws he could blow sky-high any of Uncle Sam's vessels that might seek an entrance to Hatteras Inlet." History is

kinder: It remembers Maury as the "Pathfinder of the Seas" for earlier naval pioneering.

The Confederates chose Roanoke Island, lying behind the Outer Banks and between Pamlico and Albemarle sounds, as a substitute defensive position, hoping it would limit the effectiveness of Federal possession of Hatteras. They strongly fortified the island (site of the famous Lost

Colony of early settlers) and the adjacent mainland with three forts and three independent batteries holding more than 38 cannon of various types, and added a squadron of eight gunboats. Yet this was not enough when General George McClellan, preparing for his Peninsula campaign in Virginia, decided that possession of Roanoke Island — and with it control of the North Carolina sounds — would menace Richmond's lines of communication. An expedition of 12,000 men and 19 shallow-draft gunboats, although delayed and damaged by a mid-January storm off Hatteras Inlet, captured the objective on February 8, 1862, with forces under General Ambrose Burnside.

The island today is better known for its Lost Colony period, remains of which are preserved at Fort Raleigh National Histor-

Bennett Place State Historical Park near Durham, North Carolina, preserves the farmhouse where the Confederacy's last major field army surrendered. A Unity Monument stands in front of the house.

ic Site. The 1585 fort has been reconstructed, an outdoor drama recalls the birth of Virginia Dare, the first child to be born of English parents in the New World, and the unsolved mystery of the disappearance of the colony's inhabitants. Elizabethan Gardens now grow on land once visited by violence. Near the town of Manteo, Burnside's forrces successfully assaulted the Confederate forts.

The fall of Roanoke Island was the beginning of a turbulent period for the inhabitants of North Carolina's tidewater region. Union forces used New Bern as their major base and fortified it with a continuous line of earthworks stretching along the landward side of the city. From there, and a few smaller bases, they crisscrossed the region almost at will to attack Confederate positions and to raid communities sited strategically on railroads, waterways, or roads. The rail center of Goldsboro was a particularly inviting target. While most of the actions were small in comparison with those going on elsewhere, they were intense because North Carolina soldiers were defending their homes; besides, Confederate leaders recognized the importance of the area to the whole Southern war effort, first as a source of agricultural products and second as an outlet to the world.

New Bern has a number of structures that survived both fighting and occupation, including the 1819–22 First Presbyterian Church, which was used as a hospital. Stevenson House is a good example of the early nineteenth-century architecture that dominated New Bern at that period. The town's main attraction, Tryon Palace, reconstructs the home of William Tryon, a colonial governor; New Bern was the colonial capital of North Carolina.

Fort Macon at Atlantic Beach, an antebellum brick fort with a moat, confronted the Confederates with the same type of situation the British would face later at Singapore during World War II: The fort was designed to defend against attack from the sea but was vulnerable from the landward side. Only nominally garrisoned and in poor condition at the outbreak of the Civil War, it was occupied by the Confederates in 1861 and strengthened. A year later, as part of the Federal effort to close the North Carolina coastline, the Union army occupied Beaufort and the adjacent area, isolating the fort, and secured a base on Bogue Island for siege operations. Fort Macon easily repulsed a naval attack, but it was forced to surrender after a day-long bombardment from the land that disabled many of its

Union action against the Confederate coastline required frequent amphibious operations. By the time this attack on Roanoke Island was made, experience had produced a successful method of operation.

guns — three of them with one shot. The partly restored fort is now a state historical park, and both the main fort and the counterfire rooms in the outer wall are open to the public. This provides an unusual opportunity to inspect all the aspects of a nineteenth-century fort. Although casemates are identified, only a few are furnished according to their original use.

The Union failed to close the North Carolina coast entirely. Wilmington was the last major port in the eastern Confederacy to remain open. This was thanks to Fort Fisher, a large earthworks fort at the entrance to the Cape Fear River. The surviving grassy mounds that once formed gun emplacements and protected men and powder are part of a state historical park, which also includes a small monument and a museum with a range of exhibits from a 10-pound Parrott cannon to a pair of naval anchors.

Shortly before Christmas in 1864, the largest Federal fleet assembled to that point during the war stood off the fort with 6,500 troops under Major General Benjamin F. Butler. Among 55 warships were an ironclad screw steamer and four monitors. The beach reconnaissance carried out by Sub-Assistant J.S. Bradford of the United States Coast Survey in some ways anticipated the later use of underwater demolition teams in warfare. The type of combined bombardment and amphibious operation that had succeeded at Cape Hatteras was supplemented by detonating a ship laden with explosives near the fort, in the belief that it would damage the fortifications enough to let the assault be a walk-in. Neither the exploded vessel nor the bombardment had the desired effect, though, and Butler called off the attack on Christmas Day and picked up the 2,000 troops he had landed under cover of the naval guns.

A second expedition against Wilmington the next month was the largest sealand contest of the war, with the Union utilizing 60 warships and 8,500 troops under Brigadier General Alfred H. Terry.

A diversionary attack by 2,000 sailors and Marines was repulsed with heavy losses, but Terry's attack from the rear captured the last Confederate coastal stronghold and closed the North Carolina coast completely. Confederate casualties numbered 500 and 2,083 were taken prisoner, while Union losses came to 691. The loss to the Confederacy was much greater than men, however: At that time almost half of the supplies for Lee's army were imported through Wilmington. Nearby Fort Anderson held out for another 30 days but was abandoned after undergoing heavy bombardment during a three-day siege.

Confederate earthworks are visible at Fort Anderson in the Brunswick Town State Historic Site, which primarily depicts an earlier conflict — a town abandoned by its citizens during the Revolutionary War for fear of attack by British soldiers. The town tragedy is told in excavated foundations and explanatory displays throughout the town and by means of a slide show and displays at the Visitors's Center. Civil War relics are at the New Hanover County Museum in Wilmington and include a model of the Wilmington waterfront during the 1860s and dioramas and ship models depicting the cat-and-mouse game of blockade running.

War arrived elsewhere in North Carolina in earnest that year of 1865, as the Confederacy was dying. Sherman brought

Fort Fisher, North Carolina, was so strong that its capture in 1865 required the largest landing operation of the war.

General Benjamin F. Butler already was a controversial figure by the time he led the first unsuccessful assault on Fort Fisher.

*This view of the east face of
Fort Macon shows the moat
and some gunports. Built
before the Civil War, the
fort has been partly
restored. It is an excellent
example of a typical fort of
the period.*

his scorched-earth policy into the state
after applying it liberally elsewhere along
his route. General Johnston tried to block
his path on March 15–16 at Averasboro
and March 19–21 at Bentonville, on the
road between Wilmington and Raleigh.
The Bentonville Battlefield on State Route
1008 off Interstate 95 preserves the rustic
simplicity that existed on many battlefields of the War Between the States.
Interpretive signs and Union earthworks
in quiet, mostly open countryside back up
the displays and maps in the Visitors'
Center of the state historical park.

The Harper House, restored to its
appearance when it served as a hospital
during the fighting, is the centerpiece of
the park. The first floor depicts the building's use as a field hospital, with furniture
pushed back against walls, straw pallets
spread around, medical instruments at the
ready, and even patches of artificial blood
on the floor. Other decorations are faithful
to the mid–nineteenth-century life-style of
John and Amy Harper, owners of the
house at the time of the battle.

Three hundred and sixty men are
buried in a common grave in the small
Confederate cemetery near the Visitors'
Center. They are only a small portion of
the fallen: 1,527 Federal and 2,606 Confederate soldiers died.

Bentonville was little more than the
dying gasp of a lost cause, but it was the
largest battle fought in North Carolina
and the first major attempt to stop Sherman after the loss of Atlanta. The battle
ended in a draw; but Confederate forces
found it necessary to withdraw and Sherman continued his march to Goldsboro.
Raleigh, the state capital, surrendered a
short time later.

The modest number of Civil War sites
remaining in North Carolina does not do
justice to the state's role in the conflict.
Other battles were fought at Wise's Forks
and Monroe Crossroads (Solemn Grove)
and major skirmishes took place at Rock-
ingham, Philip's Crossroads, and Boone's
Mill. Charlotte, the pride of the Piedmont,
was an inland shipbuilding center and
thus a prime target for the Federals. It was
too far from their bases to be reached with
ease, however, and escaped damage until
near the end of the war. President Davis,
during his futile effort to escape after the
fall of Richmond, held the last full meeting
of his cabinet in the city in 1866.

A raid conducted in December 1863
from Norfolk, Virginia, to the northeastern
counties of North Carolina was the first
raid of any magnitude undertaken solely
by black troops.

Union raids from Tennessee, aimed at
flanking Confederate forces and depriving
them of the arms manufactured at Salisbury, and the foraging efforts of Confederates added to the miseries of the state's
inhabitants. Bentonville was followed by
the most extensive raid into the state.
Major General George H. Stoneman led
approximately 6,000 Union troops from
Morristown, Tennessee, into western
North Carolina, where they surprised and
frightened the civilians in both mountain
and plateau cities, skirmished with small
Confederate units at times, took horses
and mules and pillaged intermittently,
broke up a Moravian Easter Week service
at Bethania, and burned installations as
varied as cotton mills, the train depot at
High Point, a small arms factory at Flor-

ence, a Confederate wagon train, and irreplaceable courthouse records. Salisbury, a major Confederate supply depot, was left under a pall of black smoke caused by burning blankets, arms, and ammunition; railroad shops; distillery; food; and the ordnance works. The raid also was carried into southwestern Virginia, where one unit narrowly missed capturing Jefferson Davis and the Cabinet of the Confederacy, who were fleeing south.

Not only were regular forces continuously engaged, but "bushwhackers" took advantage of the turbulent situation to rob and pillage through most of the war period. This was bad along the coast but devastating in the sparsely settled western counties, whose mountains provided many convenient hiding places. Unionist bushwhackers who were North Carolina natives were so bold they established a fortified camp 17 miles from Edenton on the Chowan River at Wingfield Plantation, whose owner was in Virginia. They terrorized the surrounding countryside, especially Southern sympathizers, until they were driven out by North Carolinian regulars and partisans.

When the war in North Carolina ended, it was all but over in the South. A few minor armies remained in the field in the West and the deep South, but the small, isolated farmhouse at Bennett's Farm was an appropriate setting for the end. A rural South could not compete in sustained combat with an industrialized North, and had learned that lesson the hard way.

Brunswick Town State Historic Site (left) in North Carolina primarily recreates a Revolutionary War community, but preserves these Confederate earthworks, too.

A Civil War encampment at Bentonville Battlefield re-enacts part of the last attempt to halt Sherman's drive through the Carolinas. Johnston surrendered his army shortly thereafter.

FLORIDA
Fighting in the Sun

The spark that set off the Civil War easily could have happened in Florida instead of South Carolina. Fort Pickens, on Santa Rosa Island off Pensacola, was one of the key coastal forts that the outgoing President, James Buchanan, promised not to reinforce and the incoming President, Abraham Lincoln, was determined to hold. For a time, it was a powder keg with a short fuse.

Professor J. Leitch Wright of the Florida State University's history department is among those of today who point to the similarities between the little-known events in Florida on the eve of war and the famous events at Charleston, S.C. At the time of Florida's vote on secession in early January 1861, Federal officials decided to destroy the Chattahoochee Arsenal and reinforce the Pensacola forts. To prevent this, Florida seized the arsenal from a sergeant and three men, took possession of the navy yard, and concentrated a sizable force near Fort Barrancas. Confederates about the same time took control of Fort Marion (Castillo de San Marcos) in St. Augustine from a single caretaker.

Fort Pickens was unfinished at the time but was better situated, strategically, than Fort Barrancas on the mainland, which Lieutenant Adam J. Slemmer had orders to hold for the Union. Slemmer decided to move his 46 soldiers and 35 ordinary seamen to the more defensible fort on Santa Rosa Island, which also could be reinforced from the sea — the same decision made by Major Anderson at Fort Sumter — and a war of nerves with Confederate forces on the mainland began. President Buchanan, as fearful of starting a war at Pensacola as at Charleston, agreed to maintain the status quo, and Confederates held their fire. Lincoln, after taking office, decided to reinforce the fort, however, and within a week after the bombardment of Fort

Sumter more than 2,000 soldiers were defending Fort Pickens. (Ironically, the officer carrying orders to reinforce the fort had received a pass through the Confederate lines from the new commander of the Pensacola region, General Braxton Bragg.) Confederates raided the island, and Federal guns from the fort battered Confederate Fort McRee, burned the villages of Warrington and Wolsey, and fired at construction in the navy yard — but neither side had an advantage.

Fort Pickens is now part of the Gulf Islands National Seashore, a nature preserve and recreation area so delightful that it is difficult for even Civil War buffs to concentrate on historical objects; however, ruins of the fort and a museum relate the lively history of the fort, which included imprisonment of the Indian chief Geronimo after his capture in 1886. Fort Barrancas is on the grounds of what is now the Pensacola Naval Air Station. It has been restored and is included with the Water Battery in a guided historical tour. Old

Christ Church, the oldest remaining church building in Florida, houses the Pensacola Historical Museum. It was used by Union soldiers as a barracks and hospital. A number of other antebellum structures survive, including the 1810 Charles Lavalle House and the 1825 lighthouse, still owned by the Coast Guard.

Fort Jefferson and Key West remained in Union hands throughout the war, the first because it was (and still is) inaccessible an the second because of the cleverness of Captain James M. Brannan, commander of the 44 soldiers on the island. His men were quartered some distance away from Fort Taylor, the only place that could be defended; so the captain moved them secretly, in small groups and at night, through the hostile city to the fort. What is now called the East Martello Gallery and Museum is a wartime fortification built by the Federals.

The attempt, late in the war, to take the state capital at Tallahassee started from Key West. Fort Jefferson, largest of the

Fort Pickens at the entrance to Pensacola harbor had many similarities to Fort Sumter, and easily could have been the spark that set off the Civil War.

coastal forts built by the United States in the early nineteenth century, is now a national monument as well known for legends of pirates and sunken gold as for war stories. Four of the men accused of conspiracy in the assassination of Lincoln were imprisoned there, including Dr. Samuel Mudd, who was convicted of complicity-after-the-fact because he set the broken leg of one of the fugitives. The cell he occupied can be visited.

The long coastline of Florida, facing both the Atlantic Ocean and the Gulf of Mexico, gave the state a strategic importance during the Civil War that it otherwise would not have had. The Union blockade covered both coasts, but long stretches of coastline received only intermittent patrolling. Blockading ships concentrated on the principal port areas, particularly the Apalachicola River, Suwanee River, Tampa, Indian River, and Mosquito Inlet areas and the passage between Fort Jefferson (on Tortugas Island) and Key West. The first blockading ship arrived off Apalachicola in June 1861.

After occupying federal installations at the outset of war, authorities in Florida thereafter reacted to Federal moves as Floridians were sent elsewhere to fight. About 15,000 men entered the services of the Confederacy, more than half of whom became casualties on far-off battlefields. Remote from the main areas of fighting, and with a small population, Florida was primarily a source of supplies for Confederate forces fighting elsewhere, and even this had a low priority with both sides. Ports were small and railroads did not connect with the main Southern grid; so imported products had to be transported primarily on wagons moving slowly over dusty roads. Domestically produced beef, pork, and salt also had to move overland. The largest battles fought in the state were late in the war and resulted primarily from Union attempts to disrupt the movement of supplies.

Federal troops operated against Florida's east coast from bases on the islands

Fort Jefferson's strong walls were never tested in combat. The site now is better known for its rich marine and bird life. The old cannon still point seaward, but only as historical displays for visitors to the national park. In the courtyard of the isolated fort walked some of those convicted of the assassination of President Lincoln. Dr. Samuel Mudd, sentenced because he treated the broken leg of one of the assailants, was incarcerated here.

off Georgia and South Carolina, capturing Jacksonville and Fernandina four times before deciding to hold them. Fort Clinch, which was incomplete and ungarrisoned at the start of war, was evacuated by Confederate artillery and infantry units after their position became untenable. Its tall walls and five impressive bastions still dominate the entrance to the St. Mary's River near Fernandina Beach. St. Augustine and the lower St. Johns River were occupied in 1862, and after that Union forces intermittently raided in the vicinity of the river basin, once reaching as far as Gainesville.

Raids also moved out from the forts at Pensacola. In September 1864, a Union party of 700 raided as far as Marianna near the Georgia border, where they were challenged by a ragtag group of Confederate regulars who happened to be at home on sick leave and about 150 youths and old men who had formed a home-guard unit known as the Cradle and Grave Company. The raiders easily surrounded the defenders, who threw up barricades made up of logs and old wagons, and proceeded to loot the town.

Two significant battles were fought in northern Florida. The largest, at Olustee, halted the first Federal incursion into the interior of Florida. The story of the operation, which followed the fourth occupation of Jacksonville and was conducted partly for political reasons, is told at the interpretive center and on trails and monuments in Olustee Battlefield State Park off U.S. Route 90. The Union expedition met little opposition during the early stages as Confederate leaders gathered enough troops to oppose it. Finally, Georgians and Floridians formed a battle line on February 20, 1864, in the woods at Ocean Pond, 2.5 miles from Olustee. Fighting raged for five hours and ended in a decisive victory for the Confederates. The invaders retreated all the way to Jacksonville, with Confederate cavalry harassing them. Federal

casualties numbered 1,861, as against 946 for the Confederates. The battle was decisive in another way, too: It ended Lincoln's hope of installing a loyalist government in Florida that could help his bid for reelection — one of the reasons for the campaign.

The second major battle in Florida, memorialized at the state historic site at Natural Bridge, ended a Union attempt to take the state capital of Tallahassee in March 1865, during the final weeks of the war. Planned as a combined land and naval operation along the St. Marks River,

it became strictly a land operation when the vessels ran aground. On March 6, the Federals tried unsuccessfully to dislodge a slightly smaller Confederate force, including cadets from the West Florida Seminary, whose breastworks blocked a natural bridge across the river. Four charges and other skirmishes cost the Federals 140 of their 900 men, and they retrated to their ships. As a result, Tallahassee was the only Confederate state capital east of the Mississippi not captured by the Union army during the war.

The Civil War in Florida was an occasional, almost leisurely, affair. The War in the West was quite different.

Pensacola Bay, Florida, was heavily fortified throughout the Civil War, as this period photo shows.

MISSOURI
The Bitterness of War

I t was a mighty mean fowt fight," one of the Confederates wrote home after the Battle of Wilson's Creek. That was an understatement, yet Wilson's Creek in 1861 was not even the outstanding example of the intensity of Civil War clashes in Missouri. Actually, Missouri was ablaze long before the rest of the country dissolved into Civil War. The territory's petition for statehood precipitated the great national debate on the extension of slavery and the Missouri Compromise, which admitted Missouri to the Union in 1821 as a slave state, was only a temporary solution. The attempt to extend slavery into neighboring Kansas in the 1850s bled both Missouri and Kansas, as slavery and antislavery partisans fought openly and in the process devasted a good portion of the border region.

The assault on Fort Sumter in 1861 intensified a fight that had been going on sporadically for seven years and added to the carnage. Although newly elected Governor Claiborne Fox Jackson and many other legislators favored secession, both the state legislature and a convention called to decide the issue voted against it. Federal troops under a captain-promoted-to-general, Nathaniel Lyon, disarmed the state guard and helped the Unionist faction install a new government at the capital, Jefferson City. At a meeting in Cassville, the Jackson faction approved an ordinance of secession and petitioned for admission to the Confederacy. Callaway County wanted no part of either side; it voted to become the independent Kingdom of Callaway.

Missouri men enrolled in substantial numbers on both sides: one estimate is 100,000 in the Union army and 30,000 in the Confederate army. Some served as far away as Virginia. More than 1,100 military activities of all kinds rank the state statistically as one of the most active battlegrounds of the war, even though only a few of the incidents were large enough to be classified as Battles. Union records indicate 13,885 died in blue uniform; although Missouri's loss in Confederate gray would be less, it was substantial.

The Civil War experience in Missouri was divided between guerilla action and regular warfare, both vicious. Antislavery and proslavery guerrillas roamed the state, looting, burning, and killing. Antislavery raiders thought of themselves as "reborn Puritans and their neighbors as nothing but dirt-hauling, whisky-soaked illiterates," according to the commentary at the Wilson Creek battlefield. "The Southern sympathizers were the rural Jeffersonian idealists defending their property against the wretches pouring out of Eastern and European slums." Union occupiers sometimes turned a blind eye to antislavery depredations and uprooted whole counties in an attempt to dilute Southern sympathies. Cass County, for exmple, was reduced to 600 inhabitants from the 10,000 there at the start of the war.

Regular warfare was often just as bitter, and Missouri residents had experienced "total war" before the term was invented. General Lyon, who in the early stages controlled all Federal units in Missouri, was determined to drive the secessionists from the state. He rejected pleas from Governor Jackson to allow the state to remain neutral and began a campaign against Jackson and the state militia before they could unite with Confederate units. Lyon moved his troops by steamboat up the Missouri River to Boonville and, on June 17, 1861, drove the state guard from the town in the first regular battle in Missouri.

A few weeks later, on July 5, 1861, Federal units under Colonel Franz Sigel, a refugee from the German Revolution of 1848, attempted to block Jackson's rendezvous with Confederate forces in southwest Missouri but were defeated at Carthage and hurried back to the safety of Springfield. The Carthage fighting is shown in a mural, in the Jefferson County Courthouse, which depicts the history of the city and is entitled, "Forged in Fire". Although the battlefield is not intact, there are interpretive signs, beginning about eight miles north of the city and extending to Carter Park in Carthage, that trace the events of the battle. The fighting and the damage to Carthage had a curious side effect: A teen-aged observer named Myra Belle Shirley later became the famous Belle Starr, Confederate spy and eventual outlaw.

The Battle of Wilson's Creek, the largest fought in Missouri, was not long in coming. In southwest Missouri, the state guard under Major General Sterling Price was joined by Confederate troops from Texas, Arkansas, and Louisiana under Brigadier Generals Benjamin McCulloch and N. Bart Pearce, bringing the total to about 12,000 men. Lyon, spoiling for a fight, was encamped 75 miles away at Springfield. The Confederates were eager to trap Lyon and thus regain control of the state; but Lyon, though outnumbered, hoped to surprise the advancing Confederates by attacking first.

Lyon mauled the Confederate vanguard at Dug Springs but was forced to fall back to Springfield in the face of superior numbers. The Confederate army followed and camped on the fields and bluffs overlooking Wilson's Creek, with Price eager to attack and McCulloch hesitant. McCulloch, who had a low opinion of the effectiveness of the Missouri guard, agreed to act only after Price, though superior in rank, offered to place his entire command under McCulloch.

Lyon again decided on a surprise attack and sent Colonel Sigel on a wide flanking movement against the Southern right. The Confederates, who also had planned a surprise attack on August 9, 1861, but called it off because of rain, did not reset their pickets and were surprised by Lyon's attack at 5 A.M. on the morning of August 10. They immediately lost several key positions, including the crest of a ridge

General Lyon's death as he rallied his outnumbered men for a charge against the Confederates at Wilson's Creek is depicted in this period Kurz & Allison engraving.

The temporary rock cairn on the spot where the Union commander, General Nathaniel Lyon, was killed in the Battle of Wilson's Creek, shown here in 1897, has been replaced by a handsome marble memorial.

that would become known before the battle was over as Bloody Hill. Arkansas artillery was able to halt the attack and give Price time to form a new battle line on the south slope of the hill. The fighting on that ridge, much of it at close quarters, raged for five hours; the firing was so intense it could be heard in Springfield.

An overlook on the ridge, which is at places 160 feet higher than the creek, is the prominent point of Wilson's Creek National Battlefield on State Route 181 southwest of Springfield. Looking at the tangled brush and trees, ravines, and sinkholes of the terrain from this protected overlook, it is easy to understand why the battle was so long and so costly. A map and a recorded commentary provide details of the fierce fighting for control of this commanding feature. A 0.7-mile walking trail follows the crest of the hill, where the decisive action of the battle took place, and passes the spot where Lyon, who already had received two minor wounds, was killed during a counterattack. The view of the valley and forested farms of the area is spectacular.

A short self-driving tour from the park's

Visitors' Center passes the route of the main Union advance along the creek bank to Bloody Hill; the site of the Pulaski Arkansas Battery that halted the initial attack; the Edwards Cabin, which dates from the period and is similar to the one before which Price set up his headquarters in 1861; Sharp's cornfield, where Sigel's flanking movement lost momentum and ultimately was thrown back; and the Ray House, a farmhouse used as a Confederate hospital and as a temporary resting place for Lyon's body after it had been abandoned on the field by the retreating Union army. The owner had stood on the porch and watched the battle unfold, from the

The owner of the Ray House watched the Battle of Wilson's Creek from his porch. The house still looks much as it did in this 1897 photograph.

advance through the fields to the fighting on Bloody Hill. In fact, the porch was a continuing window on the war; for four years the Rays watched soldiers and equipment march by on the Old Wire Road. After the war the house, built in 1852, served first as a post office and then as a stop on the Butterfield Overland Stage route. It has been restored to what it would have looked like in 1861.

In the Visitors' Center, a 13-minute slide presentation and superior seven-minute electric map program, with other displays, place the battle in context with the struggle for control of Missouri. McCulloch's hesitation, when a bold attack might have destroyed Lyon's smaller force and put the Confederates in command of Missouri, resulted at least in part from his lack of confidence in the Missouri guard after the skirmish at Dug Springs. The park brochure identifies another important aspect of the fighting: "Though this was one of the first battles of the Civil War and many troops had little training, on few other fields was there a greater display of courage and bravery." Of the Union officers commanding at Wilson's Creek, an unusual number — 30 — became generals before their military careers ended. A few of the young men who serve there almost anonymously would become famous in one way or another after the war, including "Wild Bill" Hickok, a Union scout and spy, and the James boys, Frank and Jesse, who marched in the Confederate ranks.

Living-history programs each summer interpret aspects of life during the Civil War, such as music and medicine.

With its leader, Lyon, dead and ammunition almost exhausted, the Federal army, leaving many of its dead behind, retreated to Springfield and then to Rolla, where it entrained for St. Louis. The victorious Confederate army, though superior in numbers, for some unknown reason did not pursue. Casualties on both sides exceeded 2,500. The bodies of 30 Union soldiers, buried in a sinkhole on the ridge by the Confederates, later were reinterred along with almost 1,600 others from both sides in Springfield National Cemetery.

On the 22nd anniversary of the battle — August 10, 1883 — a reunion in Springfield of combatants in this battle was the first in Missouri at which Blue and Gray veterans met together.

Springfield, whose citizens were Unionist in sympathy, was visited on other occasions by both sides. The town of Nevada, in the Missouri-Kansas border region that bled constantly before the war started, has a Bushwhacker Museum — named after the marauding border gangs. So much skirmishing went on around Poplar Bluff that the town was almost deserted at the end of the war. Rolla, a Union stronghold and headquarters for most of the war, was the launching point for Union sorties against Confederate forces — and sometimes a safe haven in retreat. St. Joseph, though not directly involved in the fighting, became a boom town late in the war.

There are national cemeteries at Jefferson Barracks Historical Park in St. Louis, with 11,623 Civil War soldiers among the more than 70,000 buried there, and Jefferson City, with 809 Civil War veterans. The Confederate Memorial State Park, one mile north of Higginsville at the junction of State Routes 13 and 20, includes in its 108 acres a Confederate cemetery with memorials to Southern dead.

Lexington, New Madrid, Ironton, and Westport (now part of Kansas City) also were important battlegrounds.

Lexington, a busy river port with pro-Southern leanings, preserves both the battlefield (off U.S. Route 24, not far from Interstate 70) and bitter memories of Federal occupiers, who seized nearly a million dollars from the bank. The battle was a leisurely one, even by Civil War standards, as the larger Confederate forces surrounded the Union position before making a major attack, and nearby Union units failed to join their beleaguered comrades because of lacking means of communication. It is remembered as the Battle of the Hemp Bales, a name derived from the wet bales the Confederates used as movable breastworks when assaulting the Union fortifications. Union cannon set fire to several buildings in the town and chipped a piece from a column on the courthouse. A farmer, lunch pail in hand, joined Price's besieging forces and industriously shot heads that appeared above the Union defenses until lunchtime, contentedly ate his meal, and then went back to his grisly task. Original earthworks and trenches remain. The Anderson House, constructed in 1853 and used as a hospital alternately by both sides, is preserved as a museum and contains Civil War relics and period furnishings.

This unusual battle, fought September 18–20, 1861, was a victory for the Confederates under General Price; the Union surrendered the entire garrison, 1,000 horses, 3,000 muskets, 100 wagons, and 5 pieces of artillery. One Union officer sur-

rendered his sword to his own brother, who served on Price's staff — a good example of why the conflict is sometimes called The Brothers War. Price was chivalrous, allowing the Union officers to keep their guns and horses and permitting the Irish regimental band to parade its colors before stacking arms. The Confederate army remained at Lexington for two weeks before marching south again.

The New Madrid Historical Museum includes Civil War relics commemorating the March 13, 1864, battle in which Brigadier General John Pope defeated a Confederate force.

St. Louis was a major objective of Confederate advances, and one that was almost always just beyond their grasp. Fort Davidson State Historical Park near Ironton preserves remnants of an earthen fortification with walls nine feet high and ten feet thick, which blocked one Southern move toward St. Louis. Defended by about a thousand Union troops under Brigadier General Thomas Ewing, Jr., who twice

The 1853 Anderson House was used as a hospital during the 1861 Confederate rout of Federals at Lexington, Missouri. It now houses a Civil War museum.

*Kansas City's Wornall
House recalls the decisive
battle of Westport. The
battlefield is now a
residential area, but
significant locations are
identified by historical
markers.*

refused to surrender to a superior Confederate army, it was attacked on September 26–27, 1864, by General Price. The fighting was fierce because many of the Confederate attackers were Missourians incensed by the removal of their families from their homes by Union authorities. Ewing's successful defense in what is known as the Battle of Pilot Knob, a brief but costly encounter, delayed Price's ambitious move until St. Louis could be reinforced. More than a thousand casualties had occurred before Ewing, convinced that reinforcements had arrived at St. Louis, abandoned the fort during the night and blew up the powder magazine.

Although Price's army now controlled the end of a railroad that went directly to St. Louis, he had no rolling stock to use to get there. He marched northwestward.

The battle of Westport was a two-part fight on October 21–23, 1864, that covered most of Jackson County and involved about 29,000 men on both sides. The Union's first defensive line was along Little Blue Creek, but it was easily breached on a cold, misty morning. It took the Confederates four hours of street fighting to clear Independence, however. The area

of the main fighting — along Big Blue Creek — is now a residential section in Kansas City but is identified on a self-guided auto tour by 23 historical markers and the Wornall House, a handsome 1858 home that was used by both armies as a field hospital. The house has been restored by the Jackson County Historical Society to interpret the daily lives of frontier farm families. Activities such as Civil War encampments are interspersed with cooking demonstrations, Christmas tours, craft classes, and herb sales.

At the Big Blue, Price's forces were situated between two Federal armies, but he planned to hold one off at a strong defensive position while striking the other, and then turn on the first. The failure of his defensive group almost resulted in entrapment of his entire force, and the unanticipated fighting efficiency of the Kansas militia, brought into Missouri by the Federals against their will, put him at more than just a numerical disadvantage. "Old Pap" Price, who had used only part of his 9,000 men in the battle, escaped the trap and began a retreat that would take him into Kansas and Oklahoma before he would reach Arkansas.

ARKANSAS
Reluctant Battlefield

A rkansas was in an uncomfortable position in the Civil War. It was not a priority for either side, yet it was a running battleground. More than 770 military events of all kinds occurred there, five of them classified as battles. Military units of both sides criss-crossed the state for four years, from isolated Pea Ridge in the northwest to the strategic Arkansas Post in the southeast. The largest and bloodiest battle was not even fought for control of the state but to determine the fate of a neighboring state — Missouri — and fighting went on there long after the Union took possession of the Mississippi, cutting Arkansas and other trans-Mississippi states off from the rest of the Confederacy.

Arkansas left the Union reluctantly. Although the state took over the Federal arsenal at Little Rock in February 1861, a convention in March voted against secession — but also against coercing those states that did leave the Union. After the fall of Fort Sumter and President Abraham Lincoln's call for troops, another convention reversed that decision, and in May 1861 Arkansas entered the Confederacy. As a state on the edge of the frontier, Arkansas was crossed by many trails — the Camden–Pine Bluff Road, the Fayetteville–Huntsville Trail, Mt. Elbe Road, the Memphis–Little Rock Road, the Old Military Road, and the Old Army Road among them. The result was numerous skirmishes at places with picturesque names like Buffalo Creek and Chalk Bluff. A skirmish at Rough and Ready Hill was fought 40 days after the war ended, and "the most destructive shot of the war" was fired at St. Charles when a shell from a land battery struck the steam pipe of a Union ship and killed 150 soldiers. Remnants of earthen fortifications remain at Morrilton, on the road to Petit John Mountain. Richland, a farming area that lived up to its

Along the Old Telegraph Road in Pea Ridge National Military Park Confederate attackers began to run out of ammunition and were pushed back.

name, was visited frequently by both sides; the inevitable encounters occurred, the most important happening in December 1863 and driving Confederate guerrillas from the area. Arkansas had its share of bushwhackers, too, who even burned the Ebenezer Camp Meeting, a Methodist center, in 1865.

Arkansas's awkward position in the war is evident at Pea Ridge National Military Park on U.S. Route 62, 10 miles north of Rogers. Displays in the Visitors' Center museum candidly admit that "the Federal victory here saved Missouri for the Union." Just as important, the battle marked the "beginning of the end for the Confederate hope of retaining control of the Mississippi." The museum reflects these assessments in its displays on the war in Missouri and the friction in the west. It also chronicles another unusual feature of the battle, the participation of 1,000 Cherokees and Creeks in conventional combat as part of the Confederate army. That was, according to the park's guide booklet, "the Civil War's only major battle in which Indian troops were used."

The Cherokees and Creeks, who came from Indian Territory (now the state of Oklahoma), participated in an attack on a troublesome Union artillery battery. They captured it, but were driven back when their curiosity about the "wagons that shoot" got the best of them and they stopped to inspect them. Many of them had never seen artillery in action before.

A 12-minute slide program and a seven-mile self-guided automobile tour follow the events of March 7–8, 1862, which involved almost 30,000 men. Pea Ridge was one of the few battles in which Union forces emerged victorious without superior numbers. The death of several Confederate generals at a critical time created confusion in the ranks, and the Rebels ran out of ammunition when supply wagons inexplicably turned away from the battle area. Combined casualties totaled more than 2,000.

Pea Ridge was the end of a successful campaign launched by Union Brigadier General Samuel R. Curtis to drive pro-Confederate forces, principally the state guard under General Sterling Price, from Missouri. Price led the guard into Arkansas in February 1862 to join Confederate regulars under Major General Earl Van Dorn. The combined force intended to move north to St. Louis but was intercepted by Curtis, who was dug in with 10,500 men on the ridge overlooking Little Sugar Creek. Van Dorn sent his men, some without shoes and already weary from three days of marching with little to eat, to Curtis's rear; but delays gave Curtis time to reposition his men to meet Van Dorn's two-pronged attack.

Elkhorn Tavern, around which the fighting on one prong raged, has been reconstructed and is part of the self-guided battlefield tour. At different times during the fighting, the white frame structure was used as a headquarters and hospital by both armies. Not far away, along the strategic old Telegraph Road, are displays that explain the fighting in that area. It was there the Confederates, after pushing the Union troops back, began to run out of ammunition and were forced to retreat.

Two overlooks give panoramic views of the battle site. From the Pea Ridge East overlook, approximately 60 percent of the rugged terrain involved in the fighting can be seen. A recorded commentary gives details of the decisive battle. Pea Ridge West overlook provides a good view of Boston Mountain, from which the Confederate attack was launched. A good ground-level view of the battlefield is possible along State Route 94.

Other principal stops on the self-guided tour are the graves marking the site where Leetown stood at the time of the battle — with nearby Round Top, it was one of the major points of conflict — and the Little Sugar Creek trenches, which lie in a detached area of the park just off U.S. Route 62 and were part of Curtis's original defense line.

Twenty-five years after the battle, soldiers from both sides came together on the battlefield to raise a monument showing hands clasped in reconciliation. Appropriately, the ceremony honoring the dead of both sides was held at Winton Spring, where thirsty Union soldiers had refreshed themselves during the fighting. Later, the monument was moved to a site near the tavern.

While Pea Ridge was fought for control of Missouri, the battle of Prairie Grove 43 miles to the south determined the fate of northwestern Arkansas. Prairie Grove Battlefield State Park, 10 miles southwest of Fayetteville, preserves part of the site and a few of the relics of the inconclusive battle, fought on a cold December day in 1862. Of the more than 18,000 soldiers in two armies who took part, 2,500 became casualties or were captured or missing before the day was over.

The Visitors' Center museum has an excellent assortment of rifles and muskets and cavalry sabers among a small collection arranged around a 12-pounder U.S. cannon. A model of the action is complemented by a six-minute slide show about the battle, the last major Confederate effort in the region, and the events leading up to it.

The 3.5-square-mile battlefield park has a multiple personality. It preserves the old Morrow House, first used as a headquarters by the Confederate commander, Major General Thomas C. Hindman, and then as a hospital; and the reconstructed Borden House, which was used as a vantage point by Confederate snipers — one of whom was Frank James. The stone chimney from nearby Rhea's Mill, used by the Union as a supply point during the fighting, has been relocated to the park as a battle monument dedicated to all the soldiers who fought at Prairie Grove. It is surrounded by a wall composed of stones taken from pioneer homes, mills, schools, churches, post offices, and other historic buildings throughout Washington County. Interpretive programs are conducted by park historians in Civil War costume;

guided tours are held hourly from Memorial Day to Labor Day, while maps lead visitors over a 10-mile self-guided driving course. Annual reenactment of the battle is held on the weekend nearest the anniversary, with more than 150 "soldiers" from historical associations in Arkansas and neighboring states participating. They set up a camp to show visitors how Civil War soldiers lived, and demonstrate infantry and artillery drills.

Unrelated, but occupying a major part of the park, is a recreated nineteenth-century Ozark Mountain village composed of structures brought from various places in the region.

The devotion of old soldiers to this battlefield is one of the major reasons it is preserved. Beginning in 1886, they began returning to reminisce with comrades-in-arms or to show their families where they had fought. As time went by, these reunions became more and more organized, with rides and programs, and the area became known locally as the Old Reunion Grounds. In 1909, a United Daughters of the Confederacy chapter set aside a parcel of ground as a memorial. The reunions continued until the late 1950s but became smaller and smaller, and in 1957 the state purchased 50 acres for a battlefield memorial foundation. General Hindman's sons left $100,000 in their wills as a memorial, and in 1971 the site was made part of the state's park system.

The Arkansas capital at Little Rock was a primary Union objective, of course, but General Hindman stood in the way; so Union commanders diverted their forces to Helena, an important city on the Mississippi River and the home of seven Confederate generals. Grant's campaign along the Mississippi was inexorable, but Confederates tried desperately to lift the siege of Vicksburg by attacking Helena on July 4, 1863. It was a good plan, which some historians believe might have changed the fortunes of the Confederacy along the Mississippi, but it was unsuccessful. Twelve hours of fighting failed to dislodge the

Observation points (above) provide a clear view of the Pea Ridge battlefield and the nearby hills from which the attack was launched. The battle marked the end of Confederate hopes of holding Missouri.

Elkhorn Tavern (right) was a busy place during the Battle of Pea Ridge, Arkansas. Confederate generals huddled there to plan strategy; later, surgeons worked while soldiers fought all around it.

Union forces. The Confederate monument and cemetery recall the event, and the hilltop provides a spectacular view of the Father of Waters.

The capture of Arkansas Post, seven miles south of Gillett on State Route 169, in January 1863 by Union forces and river gunboats under Major General John A. McClernand was a major step in Grant's campaign to control the Mississippi River. Erosion has obliterated the Civil War shoreline and put under water the area where Fort Hindman, the Confederate stronghold, stood, but Arkansas Post National Memorial protects the site of a smaller Confederate fort. Two miles of hiking trails lead to Civil War rifle pits and the area of the village destroyed in the fighting. Exhibits and an audio-visual program in the Visitors' Center explain the colorful history of this strategic point, which began with French discovery in 1683 and included service as the territorial capital.

With the Confederacy cut in two, Union forces under Brigadier General Frederick Steele advanced on Little Rock, which fell on September 10, 1863. Steele made his headquarters in Ten-Mile House in Pulaski County. The house was built in 1836 as a stagecoach stop and is now furnished in the style of that period.

The fighting then moved into southern Arkansas, where Pine Bluff became an early battleground. A Confederate attempt on October 25, 1863, to drive Union forces from the city was repulsed by a "fort" constructed of cotton bales, in a battle that lasted six hours and involved a heavy exchange of rifle and artillery fire.

Confederates open fire at a re-enactment of the Battle of Prairie Grove. The event is held annually on the Sunday nearest the anniversary, but living history demonstrations are conducted daily.

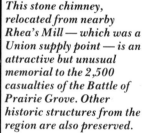

This stone chimney, relocated from nearby Rhea's Mill — which was a Union supply point — is an attractive but unusual memorial to the 2,500 casualties of the Battle of Prairie Grove. Other historic structures from the region are also preserved.

The Morrow House, used as both a headquarters and a hospital, is one of the major relics at Prairie Grove Battlefield State Park in Arkansas.

The Visitors' Center at Arkansas Post National Memorial houses relics of the colorful history of the strategic spot. Some Civil War fortifications remain, although erosion has destroyed the principal Confederate fort.

The following April, Steele conspired with Major General N.P. Banks, the Federal commander in New Orleans, to trap between them the Confederate forces in Arkansas and northern Louisiana. Steele advanced into southwestern Arkansas but, while foraging 10 miles from Camden, was met by a Confederate force under General Price. The battle of Poison Springs on April 18, 1864, was a decisive victory for the Confederates, who inflicted heavy losses and captured 200 wagons loaded with corn. The battlefield is preserved as a state park, but a historical marker is the only commemoration of the conflict there.

Steele retreated to Camden, where he chose as his headquarters a house that also had served General Price — the 1847 McCollum-Chidester home. Now owned by the Ouachita County Historical Society, it has bullet holes in the plastered wall

Bullet holes still mar the plaster in rooms of the historic McCollum-Chidester House at Camden, Arkansas.

of an upstairs room. The beautiful furniture, which had been brought upriver from New Orleans, is the only original collection from the period remaining intact in Arkansas.

General Steele was increasingly discomfited by Confederate capture of his supply trains. The site of one of those hard-fought seizures can be visited at Mark's Mill, six miles south of Kingsland on State Route 97.

When Banks's army was repulsed in Louisiana, Steele decided to retreat to Little Rock. His shortage of supplies and the need to cross the Saline River provided another opportunity for Southern forces. Confederate General E. Kirby Smith attacked, and both sides suffered sizable losses before Steele got all his forces across the river and back to Little Rock. The Jenkins Ferry battlefield, on State Route 46 southwest of Sheridan near Leola in Grant County, is now a state park and a favorite place for Civil War enthusiasts, who use metal detectors to search for relics.

Neither army could boast much about its record in Arkansas, but the results conformed to the general pattern in the western theater of war: A fighting retreat by Confederates confronted by superior numbers and resources.

LOUISIANA
Occupation

Lord Palmerston was incensed. "An Englishman must blush to think such an act had been committed by a man belonging to the Anglo-Saxon race," he told the Parliament of Great Britain, which had taken time out from the affairs of Empire to listen to the words of a pedestrian American general in far-off New Orleans, Louisiana. The Northern press was just as critical of General Order No. 28, which declared that any woman in the occupied city showing disrespect to a Union officer or soldier "shall be regarded and held liable to be treated as a woman of the town plying her avocation." In New Orleans, the general who issued the order was known as The Beast despite his compassionate attitude toward the poor and to other city problems and his effective administration of the city's affairs.

Major General Benjamin Franklin Butler's order was an overreaction to a serious problem. New Orleans citizens, who had felt secure behind forts guarding both the Mississippi River and Lake Pontchartrain approaches to the city, refused to surrender formally, although they submitted to occupation without a fight after the Union navy bypassed the river forts. Thus, the occupation began on a note of frustration, as well as resentment. Heavy-handed acts of occupation, from hauling down the state flag at gunpoint and requiring the use of Northern textbooks in the schools to ordering foreign citizens to take an oath of allegiance to the United States, aggravated the situation. Residents resisted the occupation in every imaginable way short of violence; Union soldiers were shunned or treated with disrespect by a diverse population, which was about 40 percent foreign-born but which was well integrated into the congenial life and freewheeling business atmosphere of a community now disrupted by occupation.

The "queen city of the South," New Orleans, was already occupied when this engraving appeared in April of 1862. The Union fleet lies at anchor in the Mississippi River.

It was not General Order No. 28 that established Butler's unsavory reputation. This imperious and erratic politician-turned-soldier already had become a symbol of the arbitrary rule and corruption that followed the Union army into the South and that was later legitimized by the Reconstruction era. He brazenly helped his brother accumulate a fortune in Louisiana. He was detested even by his own soldiers, despite military achievements beyond those that could be expected of an untrained commander. Butler was never convicted of corruption, but he was censured for suspicion of it; that did not prevent him from achieving his lifelong ambition of becoming governor of Massachusetts after the war.

Today's New Orleans would not be totally unfamiliar to her Civil War occupiers. The beautiful handmade iron-lace balconies of the French Quarter are as prevalent in Civil War engravings as they are in current photographs. The French Market, which Butler considered too dirty, has improved with time but still is one of the Crescent City's most colorful areas. Jackson Square and historic buildings such as St. Louis Cathedral, Cabildo and Presbytère, the Pontalba Apartments and a house named Madame John's Legacy, already were landmarks by the middle of the nineteenth century. The slogan on the equestrian statue of Andrew Jackson — "The Union must and shall be preserved" — was carved on order of General Butler. Confederate General Pierre Gustave Toutant Beauregard lived after the war in the Beauregard-Keyes house, built around 1828; the Miro House, built in 1784, represents the traditional Spanish influence. The Hermann-Grima House is furnished to reflect the opulent era in the city that was interrupted by the Civil War. Part of the U.S. Customs House, which was incomplete at the time of the war, was used by Butler as an office, and part was used as a prison for Confederate soldiers. New Orleans's Confederate Museum, the state's oldest, houses an extensive collec-

tion of relics, including uniforms, rare battle flags, weapons, medical instruments, and memorabilia of Jefferson Davis. The former Confederate President, Davis died in 1889 in a house on First Street in the Garden District, which was already well established as a prime residential area at the time of the Civil War.

Chalmette National Cemetery, adjacent to the battlefield park commemorating Andrew Jackson's decisive victory over the British during the War of 1812, was started as a resting place for men who died in the numerous Civil War hospitals in the area.

Forts Pike and Macomb, facing the Gulf of Mexico, were built after the War of 1812. Used by both sides during the Civil War, they are maintained as state commemorative areas. At Fort Pike, casemates with long exit tunnels retain the original design created by the French General Simon Bernard. The citadel's walls have been black since they were burnt during the Civil War; the structure now houses historical exhibits. Fort Macomb is under

development. Confederates evacuated the forts, about 20 miles from downtown New Orleans, after the city fell, and the Union used them as bases to raid sites along Lake Pontchartrain and the Gulf of Mexico.

The beautiful plantation houses near New Orleans, many of which have now been restored, became part of the war's commercial tug-of-war as well as the formal fighting. When skirmishing was not going on around them, Northern speculators or military foragers from both sides extracted food and cotton from their owners. Among the most picturesque are galleried San Francisco, an 1854–56 structure with beautifully painted ceilings; 1787 Destrehan, the state's oldest plantation home; Three Oaks, built in 1840, whose broad galleries with their brick columns were fired on by Union gunboats; Whitehall, now a school for the handicapped; Greek Revival–style Oak Alley, built in 1836, whose double row of live oaks have appeared in motion pictures; and Jefferson College, an 1831 structure used as a barracks by Union forces but now a

Jesuit retreat. San Francisco, Destrehan, and Oak Alley are open to the public.

The names of the bayou communities — Thibodaux, Brashear (now Morgan) City, Raceland, and New Iberia among them — appear frequently in Civil War dispatches and the diaries and letters of soldiers on both sides, who frequently mentioned the difficulty of the terrain and the voraciousness of the mosquitos. The area was a sort of no-man's-land, where the Union controlled enclaves but not the region. Bayou Teche, one of the principal arteries, witnessed much of the pageantry of war in southern Louisiana, from smuggling to land attacks on warships struggling against the vagaries of nature.

Both the Confederates and the Federals raised temporary earthen forts at Morgan City in attempts to control the region. Union troops occupied Morgan City in 1862, destroyed Confederate Forts Chene and Berwick, and built two of their own — Forts Brashear (Star) and Buchanan. The Union also used Morgan Ciy, the western terminus of the only railroad in southern Louisiana, as a major supply center and staging base for army and navy actions on Bayou Teche, against the Confederate salt works on Avery Island, and for the invasion of Texas. The New Orleans, Opelousas & Great Western Railway, which at the start of the war had provided free passage to men joining Confederate forces, thus became a major Union facility. On June 22, 1863, a daring attack by 325 Confederates of Brigadier General A.A. Mouton's command retook the city, captured more than 700 Union prisoners and enough stores to sustain Confederate forces into the next year — but held the area for only a few days. Nothing remains of the forts, but the site of Fort Brashear (Star) and the city's wartime experiences are recalled on historical markers.

New Iberia, a steamboat terminus where the paddle wheeler *Teche Queen* carries passengers much as vessels did during the last century, recalls those days principally in its beautiful antebellum mansions

— Mintmere, built in 1857; Shadows-on-the-Teche, constructed in 1834 by a wealthy sugar planter and now owned by the National Trust for Historic Preservation; and Justine, started in 1822 and added to in the 1840s and 1890s. A Civil War skirmish was fought on the grounds of Mintmere, which also served as a headquarters for Union Brigadier General Albert Lee.

As the war went on, Union activities in Louisiana were designed as much to obtain cotton for the mills of New England, where unemployed workers were becoming restless, and to enroll slaves as workers and soldiers as they were to engage the Confederates in battle or to cap-

lic church and panicking the citizens but causing few casualties. When a small group of citizens rowed out to the ships to apologize and explain that they could not control the guerrillas, Farragut agreed not to bombard the city again unless he was attacked. The next day an occupying force was in the city.

The next fighting was much more serious. On August 5, 1862, Confederate troops led by Major General John C. Breckinridge, a former Vice President of the United States, attacked the camps of the occupying army under cover of a morning fog, driving some units in confusion back into the streets of the city. Stiff Federal resistance, and mysterious orders

Naval bombardment by Admiral Farragut's fleet was effective at some places on the Western rivers, but not at Port Hudson on the Mississippi.

ture territory. Confederate forces also spent considerable time living off the land and trying to block Union access to farm produce. Nevertheless, sizable battles were fought at Baton Rouge, Port Hudson, and elsewhere as Union troops pressed deeper into the state. Ultimately, the Red River campaign into northwest Louisiana resulted in a Confederate victory at the Battle of Mansfield (Sabine Crossroads), which ended the campaign.

The fighting for Baton Rouge, which ultimately would devastate the capital, started with dirty laundry. An officer aboard one of the Federal ships on the Mississippi, while rowing ashore in search of a laundry woman, was attacked and slightly injured by guerrillas. Admiral David G. Farragut thereupon ordered the warships *Hartford* and *Kennebec* to fire upon the city, damaging the gothic capitol building and the handsome Roman Catho-

to Confederate units to halt their attacks and fall back, slowed the attack elsewhere. In the river, the Confederate ironclad ram *Arkansas*, which was supposed to support the attack, had broken down, and so Union warships were able to supplement Union artillery and provide a sanctuary within the city for defeated units. Breckinridge called off the attack when he learned the *Arkansas* was lost and pulled back to Port Hudson, one of the strongest points on the river.

Breckinridge's attack achieved indirectly what it could not do directly: It caused such concern about a Confederate attack on New Orleans that General Butler evacuated Baton Rouge to concentrate his forces. In departing, the troops — in contrast to the disciplined manner in which they had conducted the occupation prior to the battle — plundered the city.

The Battle of Baton Rouge Monument

Strong land assaults, such as this one by the Second Louisiana Regiment (composed of black troops) on May 27, 1863, caused heavy casualties but did not breach the Confederate defenses at Port Hudson.

Port Hudson was a typical Civil War earthworks fortification, but its location and determined defenders made it almost impregnable. It was the last Confederate stronghold on the Mississippi River to fall.

and a smaller marker on the grounds of the Dufroca School commemorate the battle. A 34-story capitol building long since replaced the old turreted gothic structure as the seat of state government. Burned by Union soldiers during their second occupation of the city, Old Capitol has been restored and is now a museum and tourist information center. The Old Arsenal, where strong entrenchments were built by Union engineers against the possibility of another attack, also is a museum.

Six miles of trails at the Port Hudson State Commemorative Area relate the 48-day siege and bloody assaults by 30,000 Union troops against 6,800 Confederate defenders of one of the most strategic sites on the Mississippi River. "To hold both Vicksburg and Port Hudson is necessary to a connection with Trans-Mississippi," Jefferson Davis had said. Along the trails are well-preserved remnants of the 4.5 miles of breastworks and redoubts. Among the actions here was the first major fight during the war between white and black troops.

The earthworks at Fort Desperate, a Confederate strong point that won its name during some of the fiercest fighting, are original even though they look neater now than the littered area of raw earth to be seen in photographs of the site taken shortly after the surrender. During the second attack, many wounded Union soldiers died because their commander, General N.P. Banks, would not request a truce to tend to them; the stench of decaying bodies eventually became so great that a flag of truce was arranged by the Confederates so that they could be removed. The loss of Union officers was particularly heavy. A Massachusetts soldier called the fate of the wounded "martyrdom" and said the scene at a field hospital, "here a pile of booted legs, there a pile of arms, was more trying than the horrors of the battlefield."

Confederates often risked their lives on forays into no-man's-land to retrieve the excellent Enfield rifles left by dead and wounded Union soldiers.

Other significant points on the trails are the Bull Pen, a triangle-shaped low area where Union attackers were caught in a crossfire; Fort Babcock, the most advanced position seized and held by Union forces, who pushed siege lines forward behind shields of cotton bales; Commissary Hill, a strategic artillery location during the first attack, which takes its name from its proximity to the Confederate granary and grist mill; and redoubts held by Mississippi, Alabama, and Arkansas units.

An interpretive center just off highway U.S. 61, 14 miles north of Baton Rouge, introduces the park with a museum, a breastworks replica, and an observation tower for viewing the battlefield.

Port Hudson was the last Southern stronghold on the Mississippi River to surrender, even though defenders were reduced to eating mules, horses, and rats. It raised a white flag only after receiving word that Vicksburg had fallen, making further sacrifice meaningless. The Union paid a heavy price of 4,363 casualties, whereas Confederate losses were about a sixth of that number.

Two nearby state commemorative areas hold the graves of Southerners who died at Port Hudson and in other battles in southeast Louisiana. At least two war hospitals were operated at Clinton, which also for a time was headquarters of mounted Confederate units harassing Banks's rear, and more than half the 150 soldiers buried at the Clinton Confederate State Com-

memorative Area fell at Port Hudson. In Jackson Cemetery are the unmarked graves of Confederates who died at the battle of Thompson's Creek. The cemetery at Locust Grove, with 27 plots, is all that remains of the plantation owned by the family of Jefferson Davis's sister. It was there in 1835 that Davis's wife of only three months contracted malaria and died.

Camp Moore, an assembly point and training site for Confederate recruits, stood on a wooded site on the Tangipahoa River and the New Orleans, Jackson & Great Northern Railroad not far from the Arkansas border. It was a tent city throughout its existence, and a Union raid in late 1864 scattered the remaining Confederates; no traces of the camp or training facilities remain. The site on State Route 51 north of Amite, however, is preserved as a state commemorative area whose museum relates a lively history: As many as 6,000 men at a time trained there. The cemetery, watched over by a tall monument erected in 1907, testifies that disease killed more men than bullets did during the war. Just three months after the camp opened, an epidemic of measles killed 600 to 700 recruits who, according to one of the survivors, "yielded up their patriotic young lives without having once faced the enemies of their beloved South."

Central and northern Louisiana escaped most of the ravages of the war, except for foraging and raids. However, pressed as much by political as military reasons, General Banks twice invaded the Red River Valley to confiscate sugar, cotton, and other farm products and slaves and to extend Union control in Louisiana. The campaigns would leave deep scars at Alexandria and Pineville, strategic centers on the river, and culminate in Banks's defeat in the Battle of Mansfield, south of Shreveport.

The first, a combined land and naval operation, stopped at Alexandria, a Confederate headquarters and supply base as well as a commercial packing center. Confederates retreated after only perfunctory

defense of the city, but the shallowness of the water kept the Union gunboats from going farther. Banks, who disapproved of campaigns in the Red River Valley, destroyed military targets at Alexandria and Pineville, recruited slaves as soldiers, and returned to his base. The second expedition in 1864 met brief resistance at Marksville, better known now for relics of a stone-age culture that existed a thousand years before America was discovered. This time, the gunboats were able to cross the rapids at Alexandria and move toward Shreveport, the temporary state capital. Occupation of Shreveport would give the Union effective control of Louisiana.

Banks's army of 20,000 Union men had been strengthened by 10,000 veterans of the fighting at Vicksburg, but Confederate Major General Richard Taylor chose well the place to make his stand. He stopped the campaign in the Battles of Mansfield and Pleasant Hill, 40 miles south of Shreveport.

A portion of the battlefield is preserved as a state commemorative area three miles from Mansfield, with a Visitors' Center and a quarter-mile trail through the woods, named for General Mouton, one of the Confederate commanders. Along the trail a reconstructed rail fence recreates one of the features along which the Union defenses were organized. Markers identify various phases of the April 8, 1864 battle, in which the impatience of General Taylor played an important part. Taylor tired of waiting for Banks to attack and sent his

A Confederate unit breaks camp during a re-enactment of the Battle of Mansfield, also known as the Battle of Sabine Crossroads.

A Confederate victory in these fields and forests near Mansfield saved northern Louisiana from occupation and blocked an invasion route to Texas.

General George Armstrong Custer, as commander of an occupying force, created some legends in Louisiana, too. Custer served with distinction in several theaters of the Civil War.

Monuments at the entrance to the park and elsewhere commemorate the victory and the officers who were killed in the battle, General Mouton among them. Union losses of 3,000 were about three times those of the Confederates, and Banks retreated first to Alexandria and then to Baton Rouge. His retreat added to the unusual collection of Civil War relics at the cross-river cities of Alexandria and Pineville. Shallow water trapped the Union gunboats above the falls until an ingenious dam, remnants of which still exist, enabled them to escape downstream.

The sites of Confederate Forts Buhlow and Randolph, built to protect against further Federal incursions that never came, are preserved. Mount Olivet Chapel, built in 1850, was used as a barracks by Union troops. A visit to Kent House, built in 1796 and the oldest remaining structure in central Louisiana, reveals its separate kitchen, slave quarters, and milk house. The Rosalie Sugar Mill represents a commodity involved in much of the foraging in Louisiana during the war. Lloyd Hall, an 1810 plantation house at Lecompte whose owner was hanged as a spy by the Federals, was used by armies of both sides.

Alexandria has close prewar and postwar associations with two famous Union generals: Major General William T. Sherman and Major General George Armstrong Custer, respectively. Sherman had established the forerunner of Louisiana State University at Pineville and served as its president until he resigned to accept a Union commission. Custer, sent to Alexandria in 1865 to direct the "reconstruction", faced one of his most trying challenges — the mutiny of the Third Michigan Cavalry.

The story is told locally this way. As a joke, after having been commended for its soldierly appearance, the 90-man unit turned out with hats on backward, jackets turned inside out, swords on the wrong side, and otherwise in a sloppy condition. Custer, who did not think it funny, court-

troops against both Union flanks before they could be reinforced. The Union line crumbled and retreated five miles to Pleasant Hill, where a stand by the Union XIX Corps ended the battle.

The Visitors' Center houses a collection of memorabilia, including a sizable collection of rifles and pistols, a Confederate six-pounder cannon cast in 1861 at Nashville, and good displays on the role of 60 river warships committed to the Red River Campaign. Included are models of the ironclad U.S.S. *Corondolet* and the ironclad Confederate ram *Arkansas* and photographs of the riverboats made during the campaign.

martialed the unit and sentenced a sergeant accused of being the ringleader to be shot. When Custer would not yield to a petition from the men, talk of mutiny began to circulate. Custer, aware of it, faced down the prospective mutineers on the morning of the execution of the sergeant and of another man, who had been convicted of desertion. The guns of the firing squad roared and both men dropped — the deserter dead and the sergeant fainting. Custer had ordered that he be placed just outside the line of fire from the firing squad. The site of the event is now occupied by St. Francis Xavier Cathedral.

Tyrone House, built around 1840, was spared the torch because its owner was a friend of Sherman's prior to the war. Winter Quarters, a state commemorative site at Newellton, was spared on order of General Ulysses S. Grant while most big houses in the region were burned. It was a trade-off: The wife of the owner, a Union sympathizer, offered to feed and quarter Union troops during the siege of Vicksburg. The house, built in sections starting in 1805, demonstrates two architectural styles and houses mementos of the Civil War, including diaries and personal papers, and examples of the research on cotton farming done by the plantation owner.

Louisiana was the cornerstone of Federal action along the Gulf coast, as well as important in clearing Confederates from the Mississippi River. The Gulf coast was the Confederacy's third front, where land action was light but the Union's navy strained to blockade the ports of Mississippi, Alabama, Texas, and Florida. It was an area of daring games, whether played by blockade runners trying to outwit Federal warships or amphibious Federal units trying to destroy Confederate installations and confidence.

ALABAMA
Full Speed Ahead

**D**amn the torpedoes! Full speed ahead!'' has become such an integral part of American symbolism — it was even used during World War II to stir up patriotic fervor — that it often is believed to derive from a foreign war. In fact, this example of grit and determination was inspired by a critical moment during the Battle of Mobile Bay in the Civil War.

The attack on the outer defenses of the port city of Mobile on August 5, 1864, followed in general the plan for the capture of New Orleans. The entrance to Mobile Bay was protected by formidable Forts Gaines and Morgan on opposite sides of the bay. Lesser forts protected the city proper. Admiral David C. Farragut was just as successful in running his armada past these forts as he had been in bypassing the delta forts south of New Orleans; he lost only one ship when a torpedo tore a gaping hole in the monitor *Tecumseh*, which sank head first in less than 30 seconds with her full crew aboard.

Farragut's famous words were uttered after his lead ship, the *Brooklyn*, stopped when confronted by the danger of underwater explosive devices called torpedoes — what today we call mines — which the Confederates used extensively throughout the war. The action of the *Brooklyn* at first puzzled the veteran fleet commander.

"What's the matter with the *Brooklyn?* She must have plenty of water there," he said, and moved the *Hartford*, his flagship, to the head of the line. Told there were torpedoes in the water ahead as he passed the *Brooklyn*, a subordinate later recalled, he shouted back: "Damn the torpedoes! Full speed ahead, Dayton! Hard a-starboard; ring four bells! Eight bells! Sixteen bells!"

The mines and heavy artillery fire from Fort Morgan were not the only hazards confronting the fleet. As the ships passed the fort, the Confederate ironclad ram *Tennessee* challenged the *Hartford* but could not keep up with her, and then engaged several other vessels as she moved down the Union line. Confederate gunboats also harassed the fleet but could not stop it. The presence of the Union fleet in Mobile Bay achieved one objective — closing the port to blockade runners. Defeat of the forts woule take longer.

Gunports of the battle-scarred brick walls of huge, star-shaped Fort Morgan still show the muzzles of Civil War cannon, while the bloodstains of a victim of the 19-day siege that followed the naval victory mark granite steps. Graceful arches, dark casemates, and a now-dry moat reveal both the care that went into construction and the utilitarian beauty of a nineteenth-century fort that withstood terrific bombardment before surrender on August 23. From Mobile Point, the parapet overlooks the bay and the Gulf Shores peninsula, now devoted to recreation.

Fort Gaines on Dauphin Island, a five-sided brick structure with a bastion that now houses a Civil War museum filled with guns, cannonballs, and military equipment, was seized by the Confederacy at the outbreak of war. Its guns could barely reach Farragut's ships and had little influence on the Battle of Mobile Bay; but it was kept busy by the land forces available to Farragut — a 2,400-man contingent under Brigadier General Robert S. Granger — and surrendered on August 7 after a naval bombardment, despite orders to hold out. Now the anchor and chain from Farragut's flagship are displayed at the fort's entrance.

When news of fall of the forts reached Washington on September 3, 1864, President Abraham Lincoln ordered a 100-gun salute to honor "the recent brilliant achievement of the fleet and land forces." More serious firing and much larger land forces, however, would be required to subdue the city, which was defended by a series of forts on both the eastern and western approaches. A pincers movement

by 32,000 Federal soldiers, supported by naval vessels, took Spanish Fort, southeast of the city, and Fort Blakeley after a 12-day battle in which the Confederates were outnumbered eight to one. The loss of naval vessels to Confederate mines, including two ironclads and a tinclad during the shelling of Spanish Fort, continued after Mobile was taken. Some of the Confederate fortifications and Union earthworks remain at Spanish Fort, and historical markers describe the ordeal. The

Admiral David G. Farragut led the Union naval asaults along the lower Mississippi River and on the Gulf Coast.

*The U.S.S. Hartford was
Admiral Farragut's
flagship when he uttered
the immortal words,
"Damn the torpedoes! Full
speed ahead!"*

*Powerful Fort Morgan,
shown here in a period
photo, was one of two forts
guarding the entrance to
Mobile Bay. Farragut ran
the gauntlet and defeated
the Confederate fleet in the
bay.*

Blakeley site and Blakeley Cemetery also are marked.

Union troops occupied Mobile on April 12, 1865 — three days after Lee had surrendered at Appomattox. The attack on the city apparently had been made only because it could be done. Major General William T. Sherman's forces already had left Savannah for the Carolinas and control of Mobile Bay closed the port to the Confederacy. General Ulysses S. Grant, who ordered the attack, said later he had wanted to take Mobile for two years and admitted that the action came too late to have any influence on the war.

Mobile has several historic districts, including that around Oakleigh (which was built in the 1830s) and Church Street East. Other antebellum structures include the 1860 Richards-D.A.R. House, the 1835 Cathedral of the Immaculate Conception, Carten House Museum (an 1840 Creole cottage), and the 1820s Conde-Charlotte House. The Museum of the City of Mobile displays Confederate artifacts. Bellingrath Gardens came later, but are one of the city's most famous current attractions. Spring Hill, six miles from Mobile and once a famed resort city, retains many nineteenth-century buildings.

Alabama was far removed from the main events of the Civil War and escaped invasion for more than a year. After that, it was subjected to frequent, but relatively minor, action. More than 300 military engagements took place in Alabama at almost 200 different sites. The Tennessee Valley was occupied from 1862 onward, and Athens, Guntersville, and Tuscumbia

were among the cities looted, burned, or bombarded. Six major raids, one of them employing more than 13,000 cavalry, harassed the hinterland. Alabama enrolled 75,000 men in the Confederate army, and her sons participated in almost every major battle; on the other hand, a few whites and perhaps 10,000 blacks wore the Union blue.

Civil War memories are strong at Selma, home of the Confederate navy yard — which built the Confederate ram *Tennessee* — and of 50 acres of armories and munitions plants that supplied many of the cannon and much of the ammunition used during the last two years of the war. Monuments identify the sites of the arsenal and other units of the industrial side of the city; they were burned, along with two-thirds of the other buildings, on April 2, 1865. A memorial to those who defended the city stands on remnants of the earthworks on the outskirts of the city. The five blocks of Water Avenue that escaped the torch, including the historic St. James Hotel, are one of the few antebellum riverfronts in the South. Sturdivant Hall, constructed in 1853 with a lace-ironwork balcony behind corinthian columns, is a museum containing Civil War relics.

This home was the first used by Jefferson Davis as president of the Confederate States of America and thus was the first White House of the Confederacy. It is located across from the state capitol in Montgomery, Alabama.

As the capital of Alabama, Montgomery was a natural target of Federal forces and was taken by siege late in the war. It was an emotional target, as well, because Jefferson Davis had taken the oath of office as President of the Confederacy on the steps of the 1847 Capitol Building, which remains one of the city's most impressive structures. Northeast of the capitol is a tall monument, the cornerstone of which was laid by Davis after the war; it commemorates the devotion and sacrifice of Southern women to the cause. Nearby is the so-called First White House of the Confederacy, where President Davis lived until the capital was moved to Richmond, Virginia. Although the building has been moved from its original site, it is intact and contains a number of items owned by Davis and other Civil War mementoes. The Military Museum in the Department of Archives and History contains the score of "Dixie" used at Davis's inauguration and other relics.

At Wetumpka, across the river, the Wetumpka Guards were mustered at the Presbyterian Church. A bronze plaque on the Wilcox County Courthouse at Camden (built in 1848) recognizes the family of Private Enoch H. Cook, the family that provided the largest number of Confederate soldiers — 13, five of whom were killed in action.

The Confederates were first to recognize the potential of the iron ore near Birmingham and use it to produce arms. Although the furnaces were destroyed by Union raids, a course had been set that would make the city the largest iron and steel center in the South. Civil War relics, antique furnishings, and a museum of great Alabama women are on view at Arlington House. Built in 1841, it was used as a headquarters by Union Mjor General James H. Wilson during his March–April 1865 raid through Selma and into Georgia.

Control of Tennessee put the Union army in a position to invade northern Alabama almost at will; but the lack of strategic targets made that area a low priority compared to Mississippi, where battle for the great river was being fought, and Georgia, after the decision had been made to trisect the South. Nevertheless, parts were occupied as early as 1862 as a base for further incursions. The Old State Bank Building in Decatur, whose 100-ton columns had been quarried in the Trinity Mountains and hauled eight miles to the site in 1832, shows the scars of various battles for the city. Around the dining table in the 1835 Burleson-Hinds-McEntire home, Confederate General Albert Sidney Johnston planned the attack at Shiloh; the house later was used by Union officers as a headquarters. Confederate and Union troops collided at Town Creek, and the Burritt Museum in Huntsville contains Civil War relics. Old gun emplacements whose cannon once harassed Union troops across the river in Columbus, Georgia, remain on hills near Phenix City.

Union troops met their match in the Dean of Athens College, then a school for girls: When the soldiers approached Founders' Hall, the dean sallied forth to confront them and they quickly went on their way; no one knows just what she said to them.

Confederate forces in Alabama were not large enough to defeat raiding Union armies, but one Union commander was talked into surrendering. On April 21, 1863, Colonel Abel B. Streight led a force of 2,000 Union cavalrymen from Eastport across northern Alabama toward Rome, Georgia. He was hounded by General Nathan Bedford Forrest, whose frequent attacks with a Confederate force of 600 men kept so much pressure on Streight that he thought he was outnumbered and surrendered at Cedar Bluff. It was a rare moment in a struggle that increasingly went against the Southern cause.

KENTUCKY
Key Border State

The Commonwealth of Kentucky held a key position in the Civil War. President Lincoln understood that well as early as 1861, when he wrote to a friend: "I think to lose Kentucky is nearly the same as to lose the whole game. Kentucky gone, we cannot hold Missouri, nor, as I think, Maryland. These all against us, and the job on our hands is too large for us. We would as well consent to separation at once, including the surrender of the capital." The Confederacy, too, recognized the necessity of winning Kentucky, the ninth most populous state at the time, to its cause.

Like most border states, Kentucky was sharply divided, but the division was not always what might be expected. The commonwealth had been formed from Virginia as a slave state, and thus maintained cultural and political ties with the South. Furthermore, the commercial life of Kentucky was oriented toward the Mississippi River and its tributaries. The presidents of both sides during the Civil War were native sons: Abraham Lincoln was born at Sinking Spring Farm near Hodgenville and Jefferson Davis was born at Fairview. Yet in the election of 1860, Lincoln and the Republican Party were so unpopular that he failed to carry a single county. This tangled political situation induced some big slaveowners to defend the Union, whereas a few antislavery partisans fought to defend each state's rights. Although Kentucky officially remained within the Union, many citizens were so dissatisfied with the status that they formed a rival Provisional Government, which was formally admitted to the Confederacy. The "Kentucky colonel" thus wore blue and gray with equal ease, but would have preferred to remain neutral.

Kentucky was an early and a frequent battleground:

*Confederate General
Braxton Bragg's campaign
to "free" Kentucky from
Union forces was just one of
his many wartime exploits.*

453 military activities of all types occurred in the state, but only two of them qualify as battles. A number of places lay claim to the first armed clash; but the distinction probably has to be shared by several communities, including Columbus and Hickman, where action followed occupation. At Rockcastle Hills in the southeastern section of the state, on October 21, 1861, eager but inexperienced Confederates seeking to push farther into the state were repulsed by a stronger Union force. On December 28, at Sacramento, Nathan Bedford Forrest started on the road to becoming a legend with a decisive victory over a Union force. Important skirmishes were fought at Hopkinsville, Albany, Mill Springs, Barboursville, and Pikeville. Other important Civil War sites are Paducah, Smithland, Bowling Green, Munfordville, Logan's Crossroads, Danville, Louisville, Somerset, London, and the Cumberland Gap. Camp Dick Robinson and Camp Kenton were recruiting and training stations established by a loyalist naval lieutenant turned army general, William "Old Bull" Nelson, who was later shot by a fellow general whom he had slapped in an argument. Kentucky

units served in both armies, and suffered heavy casualties—10,774 in Union uniform alone.

Kentuckians remember the period modestly. At Richmond, historical markers and a few buildings, including the 1849–50 Madison County Courthouse, which was used as a field hospital, and the old church around which the fighting moved, recall an overwhelming Confederate victory of August 20, 1862. Of the 7,000 Union troops engaged by an equal number of Confederates, 1,000 were killed or wounded and 4,300 were captured or missing. The Confederate loss was 350 men. Nearby White Hall State Shrine, just off Interstate 75, preserves the home and memorabilia of its Civil War owner, Cassius Marcellus Clay, fiery abolitionist and newspaper publisher. Munfordville, which was a Union assembly point, has two buildings with wartime associations: the red brick Presbyterian Church, which was used by Confederate General Braxton Bragg as a field hospital, and the one-story house across the street, which is now known as the Civil War Nurses Quarters.

The Perryville battlefield, in farming country about two miles from the town with the same name, is preserved as a state park. Perryville was the largest and bloodiest battle fought in Kentucky, with over 7,500 casualties, and it sealed the state within the Union. It has curiously been neglected by Civil War historians and enthusiasts.

In 1862, General Bragg devised a two-pronged plan for his Army of Tennessee to "free" Kentucky. It started successfully with 12,000 men under General Kirby Smith advancing from Knoxville as far as Lexington. Bragg moved his army from Chattanooga toward Louisville, an important Union base. Capture of Louisville would put Bragg to the rear of the Union Army of Ohio, commanded by Major General Don Carlos Buell, and give the Confederacy control of the state. Bragg would have a defensible river boundary and be in a position to advance to the

Great Lakes, cutting the North in two. It was a good plan, but it suffered from lack of coordination and was much too ambitious for the resources at Bragg's command. He counted on Kentuckians' rallying to his colors once he was firmly established, and thus providing additional forces. They did not; most of them cautiously waited to see whether he could clear Buell from the state.

The town of Perryville has a large interpretative battle map at the intersection on U.S. Route 150 where the visitor turns onto Kentucky Route 1920 to reach the battlefield. Some of the town's old structures are part of the Civil War experience, including Elmwood Inn and the red brick Crawford House on State Route 68 (Harrodsburg Pike), which Bragg used as his headquarters. The Confederate Cemetery holds nearly 400 bodies collected from the battlefield and buried in mass graves. The Dug Road, which, according to legend, Confederate artillerymen cut into the hillside to facilitate movement of their cannon, remains in use as a dirt road.

On the weekend nearest the anniversary of October 8, 1862, there is a reenactment of the battle. It began during the predawn hours on a hill overlooking Doctor's Creek but eased off during the morning as 16,000 Confederate troops moved into position for a concerted attack against 22,000 Federals. That movement confused Union commanders, who thought the Rebels were retreating, and the attack that was finally launched about 2 P.M. by men "yelling like fiends" caught them by surprise. At nightfall, the Confederates held the ridge and thus had the advantage; but Buell had committed only a third of his 61,000 troops, and Bragg believed himself too weak for victory. Thus, at midnight Bragg began to withdraw from the battlefield and soon retreated from Kentucky; he had won the battle, but he had lost the war to control the state. Bragg's abortive invasion was the last major Confederate effort to keep Kentucky in the Confederacy.

Both Buell and Bragg were preoccupied

General Don Carlos Buell's army was engaged at Perryville long before he knew it. Neither side would commit all its troops to the battle.

with political matters before the battle began. Buell, who had been dismissed by the War Department in Washington and then reinstated, was beset by command problems, as well. Bragg hoped that by installing the secessionist government in Frankfort, the commonwealth capital, he would help rally the state behind both his invasion and the Confederate cause. Neither general consciously picked Perryville as the site of a battle; maneuvering forces met there primarily because the Union army was short of water in a hot dry October and had been informed that Doctor's Creek was a good source. Neither side would employ all its forces, part of Bragg's army being immobilized by diversionary action near Frankfort. Most of the Union fighting would fall on Brigadier General Alexander McCook's I Corps while other units were never engaged.

Perryville Battlefield State Park is small, but it has a number of interesting objects packed within 100 acres of the northern end of the battle lines, which at one point during the fighting stretched for three miles. Across the road from the Visitors' Center and Museum, where a slide pre-

The strategic location of beautiful Cumberland Gap, gateway to the West, made it an important Civil War site.

sentation and Civil War relics relate the story of the battle, stands a tall Confederate monument in a shady fenced-in grove fronted by two cannon and United States and Confederate flags. At one outside corner is a painting of the battle, along with plaques bearing a map and a commentary on the fighting. A short path leads past a tall white column, authorized by Congress in 1928 to commemorate Union participation in the battle; memorials to Michigan units that were among the 61,000 Union troops at Perryville including Battery A of the First Michigan Light Artillery — whose commander, Coldwater Lewis, refused an order to spike his cannon and retreat and thus prevented the Confederates from turning the Union right flank — and memorials to General Buell and to Brigadier General James S. Jackson, commanding the 10th Ohio Division, who was killed in the fighting.

A lookout tower on the crest of the ridge provides a splendid view of some of the most important terrain of the battle as well as the fertile, rolling countryside nearby that muffled the sounds of combat so well that Buell did not realize for several hours that a major battle was in progress. A map at the base of the steel-framed tower shows the movement of units during the fighting.

Columbus, a pro-Southern community occupying a strategic point on the Missis-

sippi River, became involved in the fighting at the outbreak of the war. In September 1861, General Grant was ordered to occupy the city, but Confederates in Tennessee did not wait for him to arrive. They moved in and fortified it so well it became known as the Gibraltar of the West. Columbia-Belmont Battlefield State Park preserves part of the huge chain that Confederates stretched across the river in an attempt to block Union gunboats, restored earthworks, and numerous Civil War relics, some of which are in the park's museum.

With Columbus in Confederate hands, General Ulysses S. Grant occupied Paducah instead, and turned it into a base from which he pushed south along the Mississippi River.

Bowling Green was another Confederate strong point early in the war and was regarded as the capital of the Confederate state of Kentucky from 1861 to mid-1862. It occupied a strategic location on the Louisville & Nashville Railroad as well as on the Barren River. The temporary fortifications built there impressed Union officers, who arrived after the Confederates evacuated the city in 1862. During Old South Week nowadays, the site of Fort Webb — one of four strategic hills included in the defensive system — is often used for ceremonies. Vinegar Hill is now the site of Cherry Hall on the campus of Western Kentucky University.

The loss of Kentucky and later adversities along the Mississippi River did not deprive the Confederacy of a valuable instrument of war, the raid. Kentucky was subjected to numerous raids to disrupt Union forces, destroy railroad tracks and bridges, and collect recruits and supplies. An unimposing grave in Lexington Cemetery, not far from that of Vice President Henry Clay, the great compromiser, holds the remains of that Confederate Major General John Hunt Morgan whose cavalry units once created panic in Kentucky and adjacent Northern states. Morgan, a former Lexington businessman, caused the

Reactivated units prepare for simulated attack at Perryville, just as their forebears did. Reenactment of the battle is an annual event.

alarm bells to ring wherever he appeared. *The Washington Post* on July 7, 1863, headlined a story about a Morgan raid, "Invasion Panic at Louisville." Louisville had less to fear than it realized; Morgan did appear headed for the city as he passed through Columbia, Lebanon, and Bardstown, but he bypassed it and invaded Indiana, an act that doubled the size of his force overnight in the estimation of the *Post*'s reporter. The raiders destroyed bridges and railroad tracks and entered some towns, including Corydan. They spent more than two weeks in Indiana and Ohio and fought several engagements before the raid ended, disastrously, with the capture of Morgan and his remaining force of 393 men near New Lisbon, Ohio. Morgan was treated as a common criminal and imprisoned in the state penitentiary at Columbus, from which he later escaped.

Morgan commanded another raid into Kentucky in 1864 and captured several Union garrisons, but his 2,700 undisciplined men looted Mount Sterling and Georgetown and burned a large portion of Cynthiana. The 1,200 Federals he captured at Cynthiana were to prove his undoing: If left behind they would simply resume pursuit, and at this stage of the war Union soldiers were court-martialed if they accepted parole. Another pursuing force scattered Morgan's command, but Morgan and the largest remnant escaped to Abingdon, Virginia. Although suspended from command, Morgan moved his

Behind a menacing cannon stands the Confederate monument at Perryville Battlefield in Kentucky. Union memorials from this decisive battle, which ended Confederate hopes of controlling the key border state, are nearby.

*President Abraham Lincoln
kept his fatherly
appearance throughout the
war, despite the pressures.
The log cabin in which
Lincoln was born is now
housed in this granite
memorial building in
Kentucky. "With malice
toward none, with charity
for all" is engraved above
the entrance.*

remaining force to Greeneville, Tennessee, where he was killed.

Forrest conducted a major raid into western Kentucky in the spring of 1864, principally to obtain horses for his unmounted soldiers. He advanced through Mayfield and captured Paducah, forcing the Union garrison onto riverboats or into an earthworks fort on the western edge of town, then returned to Tennessee. A month later, after Northern newspaper accounts reported gleefully that most of the horses in Paducah had been hidden and the Confederates had missed them, a portion of Forrest's command repeated the raid. The second time, the raiders found 140 horses just where the news accounts said they had been hidden.

Parties of raiders continued to enter the state until the end of the war, but none was comparable in size. Guerrillas claiming to represent one side or the other also bled the state, the most notorious being the Confederate William Clarke Quantrill, who transferred his attentions from Kansas to Kentucky in January 1865. Quantrill was seriously wounded near Bloomfield on May 10 and died in Louisville military prison on June 6.

The Lexington National Cemetery, with 952 graves, is only one of six in the state. The largest, with 3,937 graves, is at Cava Hill, while the one at Camp Nelson is only slightly smaller — another testimonial to the deadliness of disease in Civil War camps. Other national cemeteries are at Danville, Lebanon, and Mill Springs.

The birthplaces of the opposing Civil War presidents are within a short distance of each other, and both are shrines. A 351-foot obelisk in a state park on U.S. Route 68 at Fairview honors Jefferson Davis as a native son. Both places where Lincoln lived as a youth are preserved, including the simple cabin at Knob Creek that was the first home he could remember. The Abraham Lincoln Birthplace National Historic Site, three miles south of Hodgenville, includes a hundred acres of the original farm and the plain log cabin in which he is believed to have been born, which is now enclosed in a hilltop granite memorial building reached by a long flight of steps. Lincoln's healing words, "With malice toward none, with charity for all," are engraved above the six granite columns at the entrance to the building. At the time the fate of Kentucky was being decided in the Civil War, such thoughts were far from everybody's mind.

TENNESSEE
The First Line

Unconditional surrender," as both a concept and a play on the name of General Ulysses S. Grant, began in early 1862 when the North achieved its first major victory with the capture of Forts Henry and Donelson in northwest Tennessee. Far greater battles would follow in the state, one of which could have prolonged the war; but these seizures established the pattern of pressure warfare that would dominate in the west. This and subsequent events would not only provide the military leadership the Union desperately needed but would also establish Grant as perhaps the first modern general.

Forts Henry and Donelson were part of the Confederate attempt to defend extensive borders at all points against greatly superior forces and industrial capacity, an effort that dispersed the limited resources of the Confederacy. Neither fort could survive without support; and, with Union naval forces in comand of the Tennessee and Cumberland rivers, they were quickly cut off by the superior land forces Grant led down from their base in Cairo, Illinois. In the first use of rivers for a major operation during the war, Fort Henry was attacked in 1862 and surrendered to the naval commander after most of its guns were disabled. The bulk of the troops at nearby Fort Donelson missed an opportunity to evacuate overland, mainly because of the indecisiveness of the commanders, and thus were trapped.

Fort Donelson National Military Park preserves enough of the fortifications to demonstrate how strong the fort, designed primarily to guard the river, could have been with proper outside support. Remains of earthworks that enclosed 15 acres on a bluff overlooking the Cumberland River are part of a self-driving tour of the park. In one of the most beautiful areas of the park, the overlook on the site of

The Water Battery, one of those that punished an attacking Union fleet, overlooks the beautiful Cumberland River at Fort Donelson National Military Park.

CINCINNATI. ST LOUIS. CARONDELET. ESSEX. CONESTOGA. TYLER.
LEXINGTON.

BOMBARDMENT AND CAPTURE OF FORT HENRY, TENN.

By the Federal Gunboats, under command of Commodore Andrew H. Foote — Feb'y 6th 1862.

the original river batteries, are displays of the types of cannon installed at the fort, including a 22-inch Columbiad and eight 22-pounders. In the early stages of the fighting, inexperienced gunners defeated Federal ironclads in a major land-water battle. Not far away, log huts of the kind that housed the defenders have been reconstructed.

The driving tour also passes remnants of the Confederate outer trenches, a hiking trail to one of the principal artillery positions, and the Confederate Monument, a tall marble column erected in 1933 by the Tennessee Division of the United Daughters of the Confederacy. The national cemetery holds the remains of 670 Union soldiers, 512 of them unknown. Uniformed

Fort Henry (above) was the first land target to fall to naval bombardment during the Civil War. The isolated post surrendered to Commodore Andrew H. Foote (left) in 1862 after only a short defense.

Colonel Nathan Bedford Forrest's exploits in western Tennessee, including destruction of a major Union supply depot, made him a legend in his own time. General Sherman believed Tennessee could not be pacified as long as Forrest lived.

Park Service interpreters conduct musket-firing demonstrations and establish a Civil War camp during the warm months. A 15-minute slide presentation at the Visitors' Center interprets the events and their significance.

The strength of the fort was never tested in land combat. Union forces had penetrated only about half the outer defenses when the isolated garrison surrendered on February 16, 1982; an attempt to break out had failed, largely because Confederate troops, on the verge of success, were ordered back to their entrenchments. Several thousand Confederates did escape, though, including about 700 cavalrymen and determined foot soldiers under Colonel Nathan Bedford Forrest, who was soon to gain a legendary reputation. When surrender became inevitable, the two ranking Confederate generals decided to leave with some of their men on ships that had arrived with 400 new recruits.

The loss of the forts was a stunning defeat for the Confederacy. With the capture of Forts Henry and Donelson, Grant had seized the initiative, made inevitable the evacuation of heavily fortified Columbus in Kentucky and, in fact, forced the Confederates out of Kentucky, broken their line of defense in northern Tennessee, and permanently changed the strategic situation in the west. The surrender was celebrated throughout the North by the ringing of bells. Union forces had fared badly in other early battles, and this was a refreshing change. Grant's insistence on "unconditional and immediate" surrender earned him a nickname and gave him a reputation for toughness on the battlefield that attracted the attention of President Lincoln, far away in Washington.

Confederate Brigadier General Simon Bolivar Buckner, to whom command had been passed by his departing superiors, surrendered to Grant at the Dover Hotel, which had been his headquarters. The hotel is situated in a detached section of the park and is open to visitors. Many Confederate soldiers stacked arms near the hotel and left from the landing for Northern prison camps. The meetings between Grant and Buckner were poignant. The officers had known each other at West Point, and Buckner had helped Grant out of a financial difficulty once in New York before the war.

The Nathan Bedford Forrest Memorial Park, near Camden, commemorates a happier moment for the South, an unusual cavalry-navy battle that occurred late in 1864. A monument on Pilot Knob, the highest point in western Tennessee, overlooks a portion of the Tennessee River now known as Kentucky Lake, along with part of the huge Land-Between-the-Lakes recreation complex. Exhibits in the Forrest park office highlight the battle and the colonel's superior tactical ability, which led Union General William T. Sherman to declare, "There will never be peace in Tennessee until Forrest is dead!"

At the Trace Creek annex to the park, earthworks and rifle pits are supplemented by a museum interpreting part of the battle. On November 4, 1862, artillery the unpredictable Forrest had secretly placed in woods on the bluffs above Johnsonville destroyed a major Federal supply base on the shore and sank or reduced to smoldering hulks more than thirty Federal gunboats, barges, and transports. One shell struck a stack of whiskey barrels, releasing a flaming stream that set fire to everything in its path. The Federal estimate of the loss was $8,000,000. Old Johnsonville, the ruins of the Federal ships, and most of the battlefield are all now under the waters of the artificial lake.

By the time of this battle, Forrest had established the hit-and-run tactics that interrupted Grant's supply lines and earned him a well-deserved reputation for boldness. His 1862 raiding campaign in western Kentucky, which one author has called the "dawn of Lightning War" and some experts regard as the most successful raid in military history, added to the compendium of memorable sayings that he inspired. Caught between two Union armies at Parker's Crossroads (near the present State Highway 22 exit from Interstate 40), Forrest ordered his troops to "charge them both ways" — the Union forces were so startled that he escaped with only minor losses. A tour of the battlefield and reenactment of the battle are part of the annual living-history encampment in the community in mid-June each year.

The earthworks at Fort Pillow State Historic Area, overlooking the Mississippi River on State Route 78 near Henning, are part original and part restored. The park also offers historical interpretation and more than 15 miles of hiking trails that provide excellent views of breastworks, as well as lake and forest wildlife. Fort Pillow was built by the Confederacy but had to be abandoned after the Federal victories at Shiloh and Corinth in 1862. Two years

later, General Forrest attacked the fort during a raid that included Union City and Paducah, Kentucky. Confederates drove the Federals from their defenses to the banks of the river; but a supporting gunboat would not allow them on board, and nearly half the 550 Union troops were killed in subsequent fighting that became know as the "Fort Pillow massacre." In Congress, the Joint Committee on the Conduct of the War conducted a full-scale investigation.

After the fall of Forts Henry and Donelson in 1862, Tennessee was subjected to a long period of seesaw warfare that devastated the state: Tennessee became the primary battleground of the western theater of war. Federal forces insecurely occupied the northern section of the state, including the capital at Nashville, and the Confederates created a new defensive gray

Nashville was one of the railroad hubs that helped decide the war. This wartime view shows an active depot crowded with rolling stock and debris.

To help repel the last Confederate attempt to retake Nashville, Union officers used the steps of the state capitol as artillery emplacements.

line in the southern part of the state. In all, 1,462 military activities of all kinds, at least 454 of them significant, took place in Tennessee — more than in any other state except Virginia. Great battles with substantial influence on the outcome of the war were fought at Franklin, Stone's River (at Murfreesboro), Shiloh, and Chattanooga. Many lesser battles were just as bitter, and produced some unusual actions. For example, early in 1865 the Federals used the porches of the state capital at Nashville as artillery emplacements to rebuff the last large-scale Confederate offensive on the western front.

The Civil War exhibition at the Tennessee State Museum includes photographs, drawings, and artifacts from the major engagements in the state, the personalities and exploits of leaders and heroes, and antebellum portraits and other representations of the style of life during the period.

Belle Meade Mansion, dating from 1853, and the 1849 Downtown Presbyterian Church, used as a hospital during the battle, are among the few relics of the action in Nashville. Noted for its 14-foot ceilings and classic proportions, Belle Meade typifies the great houses of the wealthy in the antebellum period. It has a

Confederate monuments exist in many Southern cities, but none is more attractive than the one in Franklin, Tennessee. Franklin was also an important battleground.

The owner of Carnton, a plantation near Franklin, buried hundreds of Confederate dead in this neat, orderly cemetery after the battle. Carnton mansion is not far away.

handsome staircase and large chandelier in the entrance hallway and is decorated in antiques. Nicks in the porch columns were caused by fighting on the lawn during the Battle of Nashville.

The national cemetery at Nashville, with 16,533 graves, has more Civil War dead than Arlington National Cemetery near the District of Columbia and only a few less than Vicksburg.

Franklin today is a model Civil War historical community. The centerpiece of its main square — named Public Square — is a tall Confederate monument. The city has numerous historic buildings, including two that have intimate associations with the war; a map just off U.S. Route 31 south of the city depicts the Battle of Franklin. The principal relics of the battle are the Carnton Mansion, built in 1826 and now gradually being restored to its appearance at the time of the battle on November 30, 1864, and the Confederate Cemetery on the grounds of the estate.

The Battle of Franklin was one of the war's bloodiest, with more than 8,500 casualties, among whom were five Confederate generals. In the aftermath, John McGavock, the owner of Carnton, collected 1,496 bodies left on the battlefield and buried them. When the wounded gathered that night in his orchard for protection against the sleet and cold, more than two hundred were taken into the mansion, where they lay on the wooden floors. The stains caused by the surgeons' amputating of limbs still darken the floorboards. Later, Carnton's owner retrieved other Confederate bodies from temporary graves and reinterred them in his neat, tree-shaded cemetery.

The Carter House in Franklin, a brick structure with simple lines built in 1830, is maintained by the state as a Civil War shrine. The main rooms of the house are decorated with period furniture and appointments, including a quilt on which Mrs. Jefferson Davis and Mrs. Robert E. Lee worked. A museum in the three-room basement, where 22 civilians huddled while fighting raged outside, displays relics, documents, and maps of the battle. Used as a command post by Union General Jacob D. Cox during the battle, Carter House and its dependencies were struck by a number of bullets and cannonballs, some of which are still visible. Other antebellum structures in Franklin include the 1831 St. Paul's Episcopal Church and the 1825 Masonic Hall.

One of the most obvious parts of the Stone's River National Battlefield is the cemetery opposite the entrance to the battlefield park. Such a location would be appropriate for any battle in central Tennessee, which, because of their intensity, were bloody affairs; but it is particularly appropriate for Stone's River. More than a third of all the soldiers involved, or 23,000 of them, became casualties during the three days of fighting that opened the Union's campaign to trisect the South. Chattanooga and Chickamauga, Kennesaw Mountain and Atlanta, would follow, adding to the carnage.

The cemetery should be the last stop on a tour of the Stone's River battlefield (now at the outskirts of Murfreesboro), because the well-tended lawns and fields and the quiet woods of the battlefield are deceptive. The artillery pieces occupying strategic points in the park, as they did when this was farmland in the strange winter battle in 1862, give only a small indication of the decisive role they played in this battle, where Confederate courage could not match the efficiency of Union artillery units. The well-positioned explanatory markers cannot convey the struggles of the foot soldiers as they fought at close range, often in hand-to-hand combat. The battle comes vividly to life at one place on the preserved battlefield: the rock-strewn woods where Michigan troops under General Philip Sheridan made a heroic, desperate stand against advancing Confederates. There, in the woods, scattered among the rock outcroppings that provided ready-made rifle pits for the Michigan infantry, are the remains of two

The Carter House (left) in Franklin, both a command post and refuge during the battle, still bears some scars. It is furnished in the style of the period and preserves relics of the battle.

demolished rifled cannon. To the troops who survived, the area would be remembered as the Slaughter Pen.

One of the displays in the Visitors' Center, entitled "Strange Christmas 1862", is indicative of the mood that preceded the battle. Union General William Rosecrans had marched out of Nashville in winter to crush the Confederate forces under General Braxton Bragg, who was encamped in winter quarters near Murfreesboro, and then move on to Chattanooga. Bragg's cavalry kept him informed of Rosecrans's progress while his troops prepared for Christmas, most of them thinking of home. Corporal Johnny Green of the 9th Kentucky Regiment dreamed of returning home victorious as he wrote a letter to his family, hoping "this joyous season would find us on Kentucky's soil with the invaders ... driven north of the Ohio River."

The eve of the battle was almost festive as bands in both armies played under skies filled with stars after days of heavy rains. This soon became a contest to see which band could play the loudest. Then the homespun westerners in both armies began singing "Home, Sweet Home."

Although Bragg held a strong position, he attacked Rosecrans's right wing at dawn on December 31, 1862 and drove it back. "Old Rosy" gave orders to "contest every inch of ground" while he prepared a new defensive line with his reserves. The costly stand by Sheridan and General George H. Thomas, and the use of cannon at almost point-blank range, bought the time for the Federals. Fighting continued until it was halted by darkness, and a silence settled over the battlefield that would continue through the next day. Bragg was so confident that Rosecrans would withdraw that he wrote to his superiors, "God has granted us a happy New Year." His exultation was pre-

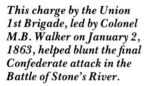

This charge by the Union 1st Brigade, led by Colonel M.B. Walker on January 2, 1863, helped blunt the final Confederate attack in the Battle of Stone's River.

mature. Rosecrans, with a superior force, stubbornly held his new positions. Bragg ordered a new attack on January 2, 1863, which forced Union troops back across Stone's River; but it was halted by concentrated artillery fire at what is now a detached section of the park distinguished by an artillery monument.

The driving tour of the park, starting at the Visitors' Center, follows the progress of the battle. Nearby are the Cedar Forest through which the Confederate attack was launched, and the Chicago Board of Trade Battery (named for the organization that contributed the funds to equip it), which blunted the Confederate attack at that point. A short distance beyond the woods where Sheridan made his stand is the area where Confederates made their deepest penetration, and the place where Rosecrans established his new line. At the only position Federal forces were able to hold throughout the battle — the Round Forest — stands the oldest Civil War monument in the nation. It was erected in 1863 by the survivors of Colonel William B. Hazen's brigade, which had held the position.

Other detached sections of the battlefield park identify the sites of buildings, since destroyed, that Bragg and Rosecrans used as headquarters.

The cemetery occupies a hillside where Union artillery stood during part of the battle. Artillery pieces, their muzzles pointed across the 6,100 white headstones identifying Union casualties, are mute testimony to the intensity of the fighting at Stone's River. Handsome monuments to many of the participating units, including the Last Shot memorial to the 15th, 16th, 18th, and 19th Infantry units and to Battery H of the 5th U.S. Artillery, provide a different perspective.

Both armies claimed a victory. Bragg won the battle but did not have the resources to force Rosecrans from the field; so he withdrew to Tullahoma, Tennessee. Another rich farming area was lost to the Confederacy, and Rosecrans had acquired the base from which later attacks on

The stubborn resistance of troops under General Philip Sheridan was an important factor in preventing a Federal rout at the year-end Battle of Stone's River near Murfreesboro, Tennessee.

Chattanooga and points south would be launched — Fortress Rosecrans, as the Union general modestly named it.

An earlier, less significant battle took place in Murfreesboro on the grounds of Oaklands plantation, the home of a frontier doctor. While Federals were using it as headquarters in July 1862, Forrest surprised the Union troops and routed them. The wounded commander, Colonel William W. Duffield, surrendered, and the two commanders then sat down to a meal in the main dining room.

In December 1862, Confederate President Jefferson Davis stayed at Oaklands on a trip to confer with General Bragg. The mansion and 10 acres of the original 1,500-acre estate form a municipal historic park that recalls the graciousness of the nineteenth-century plantation life-style. Furnishings vary according to the period in which each particular section of the three-part house was built and include some original to the Maney family, which owned the house at the time of the Civil War. Stately oaks, which gave the estate its name, are planted extensively in the park.

The Confederacy's Nathan Hale, 21-year-old Sam Davis, is remembered at his birthplace on U.S. Route 70 north of Smyrna. The home, typical of those owned

*The cannon that decorate
the national cemetery at
Stone's River battlefield are
a symbolic recreation of
reality. The artillery that
occupied this rise caused
many casualties.*

by prosperous farmers at the outbreak of the war, has been called the "most beautiful shrine to a private soldier in the United States" and is restored inside and out to look much as it did when Sam Davis lived there. The main house has square columns and a verandah, and nearby detached buildings house the kitchen, smokehouse, and slave quarters. The house is furnished in period decor, and a small museum on the grounds displays a number of Civil War artifacts, including a letter written by Sam to his family on the eve of his death.

Sam was given a hero's burial in the family graveyard after he was executed as a spy on December 24, 1863. Captured on a scouting mission behind Union lines and in possession of notes on fortifications, numbers, and movements of Federal forces, Sam turned down a pardon for betraying his source of information with these words: "If I had a thousand lives to live, I would give them all gladly rather than betray a friend or my country."

SOUTHERN TENNESSEE
The Second Line

General Albert Sidney Johnston, the second highest ranking soldier in the Confederacy, rode along the line of battle-weary soldiers at Shiloh, touching the bayonets on their rifles. "I will lead you," he declared, apparently on an impulse. Delays and stubborn resistance by Union soldiers from behind trees had created a critical situation for Southerners trying to break the Union's left flank. Inspired by Johnston, they swept forward and drove the Federals from the Peach Orchard and flanking positions before bogging down once again because of heavy casualties. It was another bloody action in one of the bloodiest battles of the Civil War. To one Federal participant, Confederate casualties looked like "a line of troops laying down to receive our fire." The most important casualty of the action would die a short time later, bleeding to death while he continued to issue orders. A severed artery in General Johnston's right leg went largely unnoticed because it bled into his boot until he collapsed in the saddle.

Johnston was not only courageous, he was an able and determined commander who provided the kind of leadership the Confederacy needed to engage superior Union manpower and resources. He was the good soldier who had resigned a western post to join The Cause. To Confederate forces in the western theater of war his death was a loss comparable to that of General T. J. "Stonewall" Jackson in the eastern one. "The West perished with Albert Sidney Johnston and the Southern country followed," one of his subordinates wrote later.

Shiloh National Military Park, on State Route 22 seven miles south of Crump, is a complete Civil War battlefield. The cemetery, historical markers, and monuments toll the 25,000 casualties and the dramatic events, and a stopping place on the self-guided automobile tour at the place where Johnston bled to death dramatizes the extent of heroism and disregard for personal safety shown on both sides almost daily. The shaded memorial area here includes part of the trunk of the tree identified later by the Governor of Tennessee, Isham G. Harris, who was present, as the one under which the Southern commander died. Nearby is a monument made up of a cannon and cannonballs.

The Union commander at Shiloh almost became a casualty in another way. General Ulysses S. Grant considered it the most misunderstood action of war. He would dwell on this battle longer than on any other in which he participated, partly because he resented the criticism of him — and of his heavy casualties — in the Northern press. Aware of the battle's importance, he would later declare that few battles of greater significance had "taken place in the history of the world." Grant may be forgiven the exaggeration; he had a personal stake. The battle tarnished his reputation and almost ended his career.

All battles are fateful; some are pivotal. Shiloh was pivotal. The Union push into the interior of the South had followed the Cumberland and Tennessee rivers, which were easier to capture than the mighty Mississippi and which provided secure and rapid means of reinforcing and resupplying forward forces. At Shiloh, the Confederacy lost a golden opportunity to achieve a major victory in the west, where one was desperately needed. As a result, western Tennessee was effectively lost to the Confederacy, which would spend the next three years trying to get it back. The inability of Confederate forces to clear southern Tennessee left Union armies encamped in the heart of the Confederate west and in control of large chunks of critical territory. Shiloh reduced the Confederacy's ability to control the central Mississipi River. A decisive victory at Shiloh would have improved the chances of holding Vicksburg.

Still, the results were as much psychological as military. Shiloh solidified thinking in the west the way First Manassas did in the east: The idea of quick victories and maneuvering was replaced by a realization that armies had to be defeated in head-on confrontation. Union forces found a new determination and confidence; command leadership was developing to augment the Federals' superior grasp of strategy. Yet Shiloh was another battle that almost didn't happen, and then was decided by Federal units that held their ground tenaciously without being aware of their influence on the outcome.

The Federal push into southern Tennessee in the spring of 1862 threatened the vital railroad hub at Corinth, Missippi — the Confederacy's only direct rail connection to the east. The object was to cut or to limit the use of that rail line, and for that purpose Grant's forces were to be united with those of General Don Carlos Buell from Nashville to create overwhelming superiority. General P.G.T. Beauregard was the first to see the advantage of striking Grant's camp at Pittsburg Landing before the two armies could unite, but later urged that the plan be abandoned because he thought delays had cost the Confederates the element of surprise. Yet Johnston insisted on attacking even if a "million" Federals confronted him, and he fell upon the unsuspecting Union army encamped at Pittsburg Landing.

One of the stops on the driving tour of the battlefield is at Shiloh Church, where the initial Confederate assault took place on April 6, 1862. Ironically, the church survived that furious combat around it only to be destroyed a short time later; the present brick church was built in 1949. Equally ironic is the meaning of its name: Place of Peace. A small pond near the church became known as Bloody Pond. It was used by soldiers of both sides to bathe their wounds, but that did not stop other thirsty soldiers from drinking from it.

The tour of the battlefield begins with the critical phases of the battle. The first stop identifies the ridge along which Grant formed his final battle line after having been driven from most of his original positions. Federal defenders at the Hornet's Nest and the Sunken Road, by repulsing four frontal assaults, bought Grant the time he needed to organize his new defensive line behind them and to man it with fresh troops. Confederates finally captured the Hornet's Nest after Brigadier General Daniel Ruggles had bombarded it with 62 cannon — the largest concentration of artillery that had so far been brought into play in the war.

The Peach Orchard comes much later in the tour, but was part of the defensive line buying time for Grant. The firing there was so intense that bullets cutting blooming buds on the trees created the illusion of falling snow.

Another critical point of the first day's fighting was the Union left flank, anchored on the Tennessee River, where troops reinforced by Buell's vanguard repulsed the final Confederate attack of the day. In this area, monuments have been erected by Iowa, Ohio, Wisconsin, and Arkansas. Other monuments on Federal Road were given by Pennsylvania, Indiana, and Illinois. The Missouri monument has the shape of the state.

General Beauregard, who assumed command of Confederate forces upon the death of Johnston, was unaware that Buell's forces had arrived and thought he had Grant "just where I wanted him and could finish him in the morning." Concerned about Confederate disarray produced by confused fighting, he ordered a halt to the attacks and a withdrawal to the captured enemy camps. Later he would be accused, with some justification, of making one of the greatest mistakes of the war. On the second day of fighting, Confederates tried to recapture that ground they had voluntarily evacuated the night before, now manned by Buell's fresh troops. The Water Oaks Pond stop on the park tour represents the major phases of that day. By noon, the outnumbered Confederates

General P.G.T. Beauregard assumed command of Confederate forces at Shiloh after the death of General Albert S. Johnston. He led the troops in an orderly retreat.

were near exhaustion; but Beauregard organized a desperate attempt to break the Federal line at Water Oaks Pond, where heavy seesaw fighting was under way. It was case of too little, too late, and Beauregard ordered a retreat to Corinth. The Confederate retreat was slow because the troops were exhausted, but Grant's army was in no condition to pursue in earnest.

A Confederate burial trench on the battlefield holding the bodies of 700 men emphasies the carnage that took place: It is only one of five such trenches at the site. General Johnston's son, Colonel William Preston Johnston, said, "No Confederate who fought at Shiloh has ever said that he found any point on that bloody field easy to assail." The National Cemetery, which overlooks the river near the Visitors' Center, is the resting place for 3,590 Civil War dead and others fallen in later wars, including Viet Nam. A monument marks the site where Grant located his field headquarters, while a pair of siege guns backed by gravestones creates a corner of appropriate symbolism. Other major battlefield points are Pittsburg Landing, now an overlook with a beautiful view of the river; the site where Federal sugeons established one of the first tent hospitals of the Civil War, an action which no doubt saved numerous lives; and the Confederate Monument.

Two headstones symbolically frame a siege gun in the national cemetery at Shiloh battlefield. Some 77,000 men fought in the battle; 23,000 were casualties or captured.

The Visitors' Center consists of several buildings and some metal plaques relating both Federal and Confederate actions during the battle. Displays and a 25-minute visual presentation inside the reception building provide a valuable introduction to the battlefield tour.

Federal occupation of western Tennessee was completed with the capture of Memphis while forces crept toward Corinth to initiate the actions in northern Mississippi that would help seal the fate of Vicksburg, the strongest remaining Confederate bastion on the Mississippi.

Grant would be involved in all of them, and ultimately in the victory in the east, but the qualities that would achieve results were only partly revealed at Shiloh. These were principally his determination and his tactical ability. He was almost naive at times; and yet Shiloh contributed to an order of battle that would produce later results. Grant's subsequent successes ulti-

mately would propel him to fame and into the presidency.

Another future president, General James A. Garfield, served in a subordinate command at the battle. Perhaps the youngest soldier of the war, 10-year-old Johnny Clem, who was unofficial drummer of the 22nd Michigan, was there, too.

Shiloh battlefield also preserves a much older segment of history. Not far from Pittsburg Landing are two types of mounds raised by prehistoric people, one a burial mound and the other a foundation for ceremonial houses.

The Battle of Britton's Lane is typical of the raiding that went on in western Tennessee during the war, and an effort is being made by citizens of nearby Denmark to preserve a football-field-sized remnant of the battlefield; a six-foot marble monument already marks the mass grave there of 25 Confederates killed in the struggle between five companies of General N.B.

Forrest's command and the 20th Illinois Infantry. Federal troops, who organized behind bales of cotton and a wooden fence, were attacked five times during a four-hour period, with the Confederate troops capturing more than 200 prisoners and a quantity of arms and equipment. Battlefield markers relate the deaths of 179 Confederates and five Federals, with larger numbers being wounded.

A related incident demonstrates a practice common among Southerners whose home areas were occupied by Union forces — slipping through the lines for brief visits at home. Two Rebel soldiers from Madison County, home on clandestine leave, were attending services at the Denmark Presbyterian Church with their girl

friends, who were of course wearing their most stylish dresses. Suddenly Union forces came looking for them. Union troops searched every inch of the church, unsuccessfully, while the congregation sat in stony silence. The Rebels were hiding under their sweethearts' big hoop skirts. The two men may really have been advance scouts for the Confederates planning the Britton's Lane attack.

The action in western Tennessee was a contest for rivers, and the object was to bisect the South; in eastern Tennessee, armies fought for mountains to effect, or to prevent, trisection of the South. While the fighting for the Cumberland Gap and surrounding territory would be intense, if sporadic, Chattanooga was the key. The Confederacy was late in realizing that; it surrendered Chattanooga without a fight, then tried desperately to win it back.

Lookout Mountain is part of the Chattanooga and Chickamauga National Military Park, which stretches across the Tennessee-Georgia border and commemorates two battles; it includes a number of separated sites. The oldest and largest noncontiguous national battlefield in the

Destroying bridges was standard procedure for retreating armies during the Civil War. Reconstructing this one at Chattanooga was a major job.

All kinds of ships, including small steamboats such as these under construction at Chattanooga, were pressed into military service.

Orchard Knob, now decorated with memorials and cannon, was a key position in the Union effort to lift the siege of Chattanooga. From this position, General Grant watched the attack on Missionary Ridge.

nation includes Point Park on Lookout Mountain, Missionary Ridge, Signal Point on Signal Mountain, Orchard Knob in Chattanooga, and Chickamauga battlefield in Georgia, where a Confederate victory began the series of events commemorated by the park.

The victorious Confederate commander at Chickamauga, General Braxton Bragg, was slow to pursue the retreating Federals after the battle was over on September 20, 1863, giving them time to reorganize and fortify the key railroad center of Chattanooga and creating such dissension among his subordinates that President Jefferson Davis made a trip from Richmond to mediate. Bragg's solution was to send General James Longstreet and other dissenters to besiege Knoxville, weakening his forces around Chattanooga at a time when Union forces were being strengthened for the effort to break out. Although the Federals were forced onto quarter rations before an adequate supply line could be established, Confederate chances of a successful siege were not good because

they could not isolate the city. In November 1863, Union forces under Grant took the offensive.

Confederate units held the high ground around three sides of the city, and this also gave them control of the river. The first Union countermove against Lookout Valley, designed to open a better supply route, was successful largely because Bragg would not believe it was occurring until he was taken to Lookout Mountain to witness the masses of blue-uniformed soldiers below. This crucial mistake was compounded by poor planning, engineering, and leadership, and by overconfidence as the Federal plan to break Bragg's flanks on Lookout Mountain and Missionary Ridge unfolded. Confederate defenders on Orchard Knob were tricked and overrun, providing the forward position from which Missionary Ridge could be assaulted.

The site of Grant's headquarters for the battle, which diverged so much from the way he had planned it that he once threatened to wreak vengeance on those responsible if it did not succeed, is preserved as part of the national park.

The flanking attack under General William Tecumseh Sherman was an utter failure; but it produced an 18-year-old winner of the Congressional Medal of Honor by the name of Arthur MacArthur, who later became a famous general but whose son, Douglas, was destined to become even more famous as commander in the Pacific during World War II and the Korean conflict.

The assault on Lookout Mountain directed by General Joseph Hooker was successful, but it was the frontal assault against Missionary Ridge, intended as a diversion, that swept uncontrolled beyond its limited objective to capture the ridge and drive the Confederates from the field.

Park sites along the scenic drive on Missionary Ridge include the place where Confederate soldiers repulsed Sherman's repeated attacks, and other critical points now identified by plaques and by cannon of that era. Many of the 5,824 Federals who died in the battle lie in the city's National Cemetery on Bailey Avenue. Confederate losses totaled 6,667 ' ' ding 4,146 missing.

Lookout Mountain, which dominates the Moccasin Bend of the Tennessee River, is a hodgepodge of tourist attractions, including Ruby Falls and Rock City, with Point Park and the Cravens House at the end of a scenic drive up the steep slopes. Both the drive and visits to the park and house provide an insight into the difficulty of the Federals's task of clearing Confederates from the slopes.

From Point Park on the crest, three batteries of Napoleons and Parrott cannon point toward the city and the valley. The tall New York Peace Memorial is topped by soldiers of both sides shaking hands under one flag, and the Ochs museum and Overlook relate, through pictures and exhibits, the story and significance of the fighting for Chattanooga. The white two-story frame Cravens House, used as a Confederate headquarters, was badly damaged by some of the fiercest fighting

on the slopes; it has been restored to depict how people lived in that period, with hostesses in costume to complete the picture. Park rangers demonstrate weapons and equipment during the warm months. A number of hiking trails extend from the principal Bluff Trail, which goes down the mountain from the Ochs overlook.

The three Union divisions attacking Lookout Mountain greatly outnumbered the Confederates. Artillerymen on the heights could not see through the morning fog — later, the event became known as the Battle Above the Clouds — but Union forces could not dislodge the Southerners. After darkness, however, the Confederates withdrew from this exposed position.

Exhibits on two acres of Signal Mountain, which gets its name from its use as a Civil War signaling station, explain other aspects of the fighting. Additional monuments stand along the highways of the region, including those leading to Chickamauga in Georgia. The "Confederama" on Lookout Mountain uses more than 5,000 miniature soldiers and weapons, combined with flashing lights, battle sounds, and smoke, to recreate the four principal battles that took place in the Chatanooga area; the attraction is billed as the world's largest battlefield display, covering 480 square feet.

Conflict in eastern Tennessee, which went on intermittently throughout the war, was seldom coordinated with action in the more strategic middle and western areas of the state, yet the fate of this mountainous region was usually determined by events elsewhere, and in particular the battle for Chattanooga. If the Confederates had taken the city, Union forces in east Tennessee, commanded by General Ambrose Burnside, would have been outflanked and exposed; and the meager Confederate forces operating there might have prevailed, even though the residents of the region were predominately Unionist in sympathy and enrolled perhaps as many as 30,000 men in the Union army.

East Tennessee was also the home of

(Overleaf) The crest of Lookout Mountain, now part of the national battlefield park, overlooks Chattanooga. A Union attack on the fortified hill failed, but success elsewhere forced the Confederates to abandon it.

Abraham Lincoln's second-term Vice President, Andrew Johnson, who became President when Lincoln was assassinated and survived impeachment in the tug-of-war over treatment of the defeated South.

Battles in eastern Tennessee were usually small and sometimes confused encounters, and few of the battlegrounds have been preserved. There are, however, a number of relics scattered westward from the Cumberland Gap, which was the major objective of much of the fighting.

Cumberland Gap National Historical Park lies over the major route through the mountains by which early settlers reached the west. Its strategic value during the Civil War is acknowledged with a display of Civil War weapons at the Visitors' Center and a few preserved rifle pits. Knoxville, occupied by the Union for much of the war, recalls that era at Confederate Memorial Hall and at the antebellum Bleak House, which General Longstreet used as his headquarters during his unsuccessful 1863 attempt to evict Burnside. The Armstrong-Lockett House dates from 1834. Among the 2,109 Federal casualties buried in Knoxville National Cemetery, 1,046 are unknown.

Hale Springs Inn was erected in 1834 on a major stagecoach route. It bears reminders of the shifting fortunes of Rogersville: Trap doors probably were installed by owners to provide a quick means of hiding silverware and other valuables every time the city changed hands. The inn was headquarters when Union forces were in town; Confederates preferred to use the Kyle House across the street when they were in control.

Lincoln Memorial University in Harrogate, established after the war by Union Major General O.O. Howard, who had been impressed by the patriotism of the people of the region, has a sizable collection of Civil War memorabilia among items related to its namesake.

Dandridge, 30 miles east of Knoxville, was saved for the Confederacy by a mistake of the U.S. Army Corps of Engineers. A Union army foraging in the area and a Confederate force wintering at Russellville engaged in inconclusive skirmishing along the French Broad River in January 1864. Union forces completed what they thought was a bridge across the river and sent cavalry charging across — only to discover that the bridge ended on an island in the stream. Embarrassed Union troopers withdrew the next day. In 1984, as part of the 192nd Founding Festival of Jefferson County, the skirmishing was reenacted by reactivated Civil War units from Tennessee, Texas, Florida, Ohio, and Michigan.

Memories of Andrew Johnson, the only American president to be impeached, are strong in Greenville, his home town after the age of 17. Three separate areas — his home, the tailor shop he operated, and his grave in the National Cemetery — make up the Andrew Johnson National Historic Site. The one-room tailor shop remains in its original location but is enclosed in a brick building, which also houses other relics. The two-story brick home where Johnson lived after 1851 while not in Washington holds many mementos of his political career as Congressman, Senator, Vice President, and President, and as military governor of Tennessee during the war. The 25-foot-high monument at his gravesite incorporates an American eagle poised for flight and a scroll depicting the Constitution of the United States. His epitaph is: "His faith in the people never wavered."

MISSISSIPPI
Control of the River

Vicksburg National Military Park in Mississippi, populated with handsome memorials, preserved fortifications, and other memories of the decisive siege, is one of the most impressive Civil War battlefields. Vicksburg was the key to control of the Mississippi and in Union President Abraham Lincoln's view, the war could "never be brought to a close until that key is in our pocket." Pocketing the key would require heavy casualties and inflict untold hardship upon besieged and besieger alike — but in reality the fate of Vicksburg was decided before the siege began. Indecisiveness, conflicting orders, an appalling lack of intelligence information, and bad judgment enabled Grant to ravage Vicksburg's natural support areas and invest the town from its vulnerable rear.

The fall of Vicksburg began with a fortress mentality, as Confederate Lieutenant General John C. Pemberton demanded reinforcements but did not appreciate the necessity of an active defense; it was abetted by division of forces at a time when concentration might have destroyed Grant's army; and it was confirmed by belated efforts, with inadequate forces, to rectify earlier mistakes.

The first attempts by General Ulysses S. Grant to capture Vicksburg from the north were dismal failures, largely because of impossible terrain. He then spent thousands of man-hours in futile attempts to dig canals through the marshes on the Louisiana side of the Mississipi River in an effort to avoid the well-situated Confederate guns on the heights above the river at Vicksburg. He finally decided to divide his forces and attack the city from the south and east. Confederate General Joseph E. Johnston ordered Pemberton to concentrate his forces and strike Grant.

"If Grant's army lands on this side of the river, the safety of Mississippi depends on beating it," Johnston wired

Pemberton. "For that object you should unite your whole force."

This good advice went unheeded, and Johnston tried again with a similar order, adding, "success will give you back what you abandoned to win it." But Pemberton had orders from Confederate President Jefferson Davis to hold Vicksburg, and he sent inadequate forces to stop Grant.

One of the most famous raids of the war, led by Colonel B.H. Grierson from Tennessee through the heart of Mississippi to Baton Rouge, Louisiana, was a spectacular diversion while Grant moved his forces southward on the Louisiana shore of the Mississippi. Grierson's 17-day raid was just as successful as Hollywood later portrayed it, destroying railroads and other military targets and generally evading Confederate pursuers along a 800-mile route.

Grand Gulf Military Monument, 10 miles northwest of Port Gibson off U.S. Route 61, preserves the site of a successful attempt on April 29, 1863, to stop Grant from crossing to the east side of the river. The Civil War left Grand Gulf a virtual ghost town, and it was not until 1962 that the strategic importance of its location was recognized by the dedication of the memorial park. Exhibits and relics, including remnants of Fort Coburn and Fort Wade, trace the fighting at Grand Gulf, where the Union suffered heavy losses without dislodging the defenders under Brigadier General John S. Bowen. Photographs, maps, scale models, uniforms, muskets, cannonballs, and artifacts recovered in the area are displayed in a museum. Authentic buildings from the region include a frame church and a water mill. Hiking trails and an observation tower, from which miles of the Mississippi River are visible, provide an overview of the battle area and of the lush countryside.

Grant responded to the stalwart defense

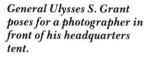

General Ulysses S. Grant poses for a photographer in front of his headquarters tent.

Confederate General John S. Bowen directed the slashing attack at Champion Hill, Mississippi. This monument is at Vicksburg National Battlefield.

of Grand Gulf by moving farther south and attacking Port Gibson, where an outnumbered brigade could not stop his advance. The Shaffer House near Port Gibson, built about 1840, survived the fighting; but Port Gibson's best-known structure is the 1859 Presbyterian church, whose steeple is topped by a gilded hand pointing toward heaven. Confederate Major General Earl Van Dorn is buried in Wintergreen Cemetery, facing south, along with both Confederate and Union casualties from the Battle of Port Gibson. Other antebellum structures include St. Joseph's Roman Catholic Church of 1849, the 1860 Methodist church, the Idlewild mansion, dating from 1833, "Miss Phoebe's" from 1811, and the Disharoon House, raised in the 1830s and known for its unusual staircase and chandeliers from the steam boat *Robert E. Lee*. Of the plantation house at Windsor, 12 miles southwest of Port Gibson on Mississippi Route 552, only the handsome columns remain. It was not destroyed by war, although the mansion was used as an observation post by the Confederates and as a hospital by the Union; it survived the war only to burn in 1890.

The Battle of Raymond, a town now listed as a stop along the scenic Natchez Trace Parkway that connects many Mississippi Civil War sites, was an example of how Pemberton sent inadequate forces to confront Grant and yet of how effective the Southern philosophy of attack could be: In the smoke and dust that enveloped the battlefield on May 12, 1863, a Confederate brigade stymied an entire Union corps for half a day by repeated attacks. In the end, the greater numbers prevailed; and the first Federals into Raymond, the 20th Ohio, sat down to a picnic the ladies of the town had prepared in anticipation of a Confederate victory.

As Grant marched to destroy Jackson (where the 1857 Manship House, The Oaks, built in 1846, and the 1842 Governor's Mansion are among the few buildings to survive), Pemberton missed an opportunity to catch him between two armies and perhaps destroy him. When he finally confronted Grant at Champion Hill and Big Black River, it was a case of "too little, too late." Bowen's slashing attack over the rugged terrain at Champion Hill during the May 16 battle, which bent but could not break Grant's line, has left a legacy that includes a gray-clad ghost and an annual reenactment of the battle at Edwards under the auspices of the Champion Hill Battlefield Foundation. Pember-

ton held the bridges at the Big Black until it was obvious his rear guard had been cut off, then retreated inside his strong fortifications at Vicksburg.

The Vicksburg battlefield park stretches in an irregular arc across the hills around the city of Vicksburg, its northern flank resting — as it did then — on the water. The museum in the Visitors' Center shows both the military and the human sides of the siege, the culmination of a year of bloody campaigning by Grant to take the

Confederacy's greatest Mississippi River stronghold. A mock-up of the caves where civilians lived to escape the Union bombardment is outfitted with sparse household furnishings. Displays show the meager rations soldiers and civilians alike received — in the latter stage of the siege, a one-day ration consisted of two biscuits, two portions of bacon, a few peas, and a spoonful of rice. The defenders of Vicksburg endured these deprivations for 47 days. Among other displays are a mortar

Grant's two attacks on Vicksburg, one of which is depicted in this contemporary print, were unsuccessful. The city finally was taken by siege.

Even though the massed artillery at Vicksburg is silent now, it still attests to the fierceness of the struggles that took place there.

and cannonballs, carbines, muskets, swords, and a mock-up of a Confederate hospital room. An audio-visual presentation details both Grant's initial efforts to break the Confederate lines, under the false impression Pemberton's troops had been demoralized at Champion Hill and the Big Black, and the siege that followed.

A 16-mile drive, starting at the Visitors' Center, traverses sections of the Union siege line and the Confederate defenses; 1,400 monuments, ranging from a classical domed building to simple marble tablets, can be seen. The roller-coaster road passes through a memorial arch and follows the wooded contours of the hills along the Union siege line and then the Confederate defenses. Artillery batteries are placed at numerous places, on their original sites, and memorials and statues stand on forts, redans, lunettes, breastworks, and other features of the terrain associated with various units.

The classical lines of the domed white Illinois memorial make it the most beautiful in the park, while the Alabama monument and others boast sculptures on traditional columns. The white frame Shirley House, the only surviving wartime structure in the park, is restored to its 1863 appearance, when it served as a headquarters for the 45th Illinois Infantry. Missouri, which had sons fighting on both sides, raised a monument commemorating both. Fort Hill, which anchored the Confederate left and was so formidable that no Union attack was even made against it, provides the best view of the countryside and river. Stockade Redan, which guarded one of the roads into Vicksburg, was a focal point for Grant's two attempts — on May 19 and 22 — to storm the fortifications. The second attempt, an all-out attack along a three-mile front, may have been the first use of clockwork to time an attack, but it failed at a cost of 502 Union lives. During the siege, Federal forces tried a tactic that would lead to disaster later at Petersburg, Virginia — digging mines under Confederate forts and detonating explosives. At Vicksburg, two unsuccessful attempts were made against the Third Louisiana Redan.

The site where Grant and Pemberton, who had been comrades-in-arms during the Mexican War nearly 20 years earlier, met to discuss surrender terms is on Pemberton Avenue. It was the first place to be marked — on July 4, 1863 — but souvenir hunters chipped two successive marble monuments so badly, they were replaced by a cannon.

Grant at first demanded unconditional surrender, but decided to soften the terms after Pemberton refused to accept such harsh conditions. At 10 A.M. on July 4 — Independence Day — Vicksburg was formally surrendered as the Confederates stacked arms and relinquished their colors. Five days later, when Port Hudson surrendered, the Confederacy was divided. Lincoln could proclaim that "the Father of Waters again goes unvexed to the sea."

Lincoln's comment recognized the important role of naval power on the rivers in the western theater of war. Memorials are few because so few relics remain. At long last, that aspect of the war is now being

Fort Massachusetts, located on Ship Island in the Gulf of Mexico, remained in Union hands and was a valuable staging area for the invasion of Mobile and other coastal points.

explored in a museum at Vicksburg national park that includes a partial reconstruction of the gunboat U.S.S. *Cairo,* incorporating a 15-ton section of the bow and other artifacts recovered from the bottom of the river. The life of the sailors is shown through personal effects and weapons, such recovered equipment as mess gear and ship fittings, and photographs of Mississippi warships and their crews. Audio-visual presentations relate how the *Cairo* sank in 12 minutes — without loss of a single life — and the modern tale of how the parts were found and recovered.

The city of Vicksburg preserves its own memories of the war, with downtown memorials and strategically placed cannon overlooking the waterfront — which now is actually the type of canal Grant tried to build in other areas because the fickle river changed its course away from the city after the war. Among the remaining antebellum residences are Cedar Grove, damaged by warship bombardment during the siege; the 1835 Balfour House, where a Christmas Eve ball was interrupted by the arrival of Union gunboats heralding the siege

and which was used as a Union headquarters after the surrender of the city; Anchuca, built about 1830 and reportedly a platform from which the Confederate President delivered a speech; six acres of gardens around Great Oaks, built in the 1830s; and the Old Courthouse Museum, whose iron doors and 30-foot columns complement more than 10,000 exhibits.

Fighting in Mississippi did not begin or end with the destruction of Jackson and the fall of Vicksburg. Ship Island, now part of the Gulf Coast National Seashore, was occupied in 1862 by Federal troops who used Fort Massachusetts (now restored to its Civil War appearance) as a base to invade Mobile, Alabama, and other coastal areas.

Beauvoir mansion, near Biloxi, is preserved as a shrine to the memory of Jefferson Davis, who lived here for 10 years after being released from Union prisons; it was here he wrote *The Rise and Fall of the Confederate Government.* The Tomb of the Unknown Soldier of the Confederate States is situated in the cemetery on the grounds. Holly Springs, where more than

*Beauvoir, near Biloxi,
Mississippi, was Jefferson
Davis's last home. It holds
many relics of the
Confederate president and
his family.*

a hundred historic homes are preserved, changed hands 60 times during the war and was the scene of a successful Confederate raid on Grant's supplies.

Many of the superb antebellum homes of Natchez survived the war, including Rosalie, which was used for a time as a Union headquarters, and Dunleith, a

stately Greek Revival house with colonnaded galleries, completed around 1856. The city of Columbus says the first Memorial Day was observed there in 1886, when the ladies of the city placed flowers on the graves of 1,500 Confederate and Union soldiers who died at Shiloh.

Two significant battles in the Tupelo

area in 1864 are memorialized by one-acre battlefield parks, monuments, maps, and historical artifacts. At Brice's Crossroads National Battlefield Site, on state Route 370 northwest of Tupelo, General N.B. Forrest defeated a Federal army, under Brigadier General Samuel D. Sturgis, that outnumbered him more than two to one. Five weeks later, armies under Confederate Brigadier General Stephen D. Lee and Union Brigadier General Andrew J. Smith fought an inconclusive battle on land now inside the city, part of which is preserved as the Tupelo National Battlefield. The Tupelo Museum includes Civil War relics among its exhibits.

Corinth, three miles from the Tennessee border and the junction of two railroads, was lost soon after the Battle of Shiloh, but Confederate forces tried unsuccessfully to recapture it in a hard-fought battle on October 3–4, 1862. The 1857 Curlee House, used as headquarters by three generals, is now a museum. The earth-works of Battery Robinett, the most hotly contested point in the battle, is the main feature of the city's battlefield park. The Union redoubt was assaulted by 2,000 Confederates, whose advance caused one defender to exclaim, "In all of my campaigning, I had never seen anything so hard to stand as that slow, steady tramp." The Confederates breached the position to silence its three Parrott cannon, but could not hold their gains. The park also has a tall monument to Colonel William P. Rogers, who led the third and final assault and whose last words to his Texas soldiers were, "Men, save yourselves or sell your lives as dear as possible." Other memorials, historical markers, and period cannon complete the story of one of the longest and most costly battles in the Western theater of war. In the national cemetery, in another section of the city, 5,719 soldiers, 3,937 of them unknown, lie near a metal plaque bearing Lincoln's Gettysburg Address.

GEORGIA
The March to the Sea

Thanks to Margaret Mitchell, whose novel *Gone With the Wind* became a popular motion picture, Georgia's role in the Civil War is perceived as being much greater than it was. Of course the battles fought at Chickamauga and Kennesaw Mountain were of epic proportions and the burning of Atlanta was spectacular, but the period of death and destruction in the South's richest and most populous state was brief compared to that of the front-line states of Virginia and Tennessee and the annex war along the Mississippi.

The Union strategies of dividing the Confederacy at the Mississippi and of conquering the Confederate capital at Richmond, even the effort to strangle the South by blockading all its ports, including those in Georgia, existed almost from the beginning of the war. The decision to trisect the South came later, after the early effort at holding the border states and occupying Tennessee had succeeded. The battle at Chickamauga, which is barely inside the Georgia boundary, did not occur until September 1863, and the state escaped major harm until 1864.

Geogia's late arrival in the devastation derby meant that it felt the full force of a battle-hardened Federal army and a war-weary Union, ready to accept wanton destruction and the excesses and improprieties committed by individual soldiers in exchange for an earlier end to the fighting. Furthermore, Federal officers throughout the war demonstrated little talent for maintaining discipline among their soldiers in conquered territory. Thus, the accumulated force of the war fell particularly hard on Georgia, and Sherman's March to the Sea has become a symbol of destructiveness. It was also a forerunner of the modern concept of "total war".

Historians at the battlefields try to demonstrate both the heroics of combat and the futility of war; but this is difficult in the serenity of park settings, where visitors from both north and south come as much to relax as to experience vicariously the deeds of their ancestors. However, the difficult terrain of northwest Georgia, where the two largest and most decisive battles were fought, combine with cherished memorials and with the stark reality of large Civil War graveyards at Andersonville and Marietta to create a balanced perspective.

Some historians contend the South almost won the war at the Battle of Chickamauga. A decisive victory for the Confederacy after a string of defeats and retreats in the west, it could have had far-reaching consequences if General Braxton Bragg had aggressively pursued the demoralized and retreating Union army under General William Rosecrans. But Bragg was cautious by nature and rejected the pleas of his subordinates that quick and forceful action might make Rosecrans abandon all of Tennessee and thus fan antiwar sentiment in the North. When Bragg finally followed — four days later — Rosecrans was entrenched in Chattanooga, with reinforcements on the way and General Ulysses S. Grant soon to take charge. While it is doubtful the South could have overcome Northern superiority in manpower and industrial capacity under any circum-

stances, a successful follow-up after Chickamauga would have changed the strategic situation in the west so much that it could have lengthened the war.

The battlefield at Chickamauga possesses a balance of beauty and solemnity. Memorials and historic places along the seven-mile self-guided driving tour are unobtrusively set in sylvan settings. This is appropriate because most of the battle was fought in forests. The long-silent cannon, which joggers now use for limbering-up exercises, are poignant visual reminders of the "thunder of cannon" that erupted along the quiet lanes on a September day in 1863. One historical marker totals the 34,000 casualties of the two-day "sluggish river of death," as Confederate Major General William Bate described the Chickamauga battle. The 22nd Alabama lost 55 percent of its men.

Buildings on the battlefield, even the white-columned Visitors' Center, contribute to a relaxed atmosphere. The audiovisual presentation is a 20-minute capsule of the overall strategy of the war, including the Chickamauga and Chattanooga battles. The largest section of the museum, an excellent collection of rifles from the Civil War and earlier, details the innovations made in firearms, both domestic and imported, during the war. Great Britain sold more weapons to both sides than any other country. Whereas the musket was the principal shoulder weapon of the war, more varieties of guns were used — partly because of necessity — than in any other conflict. Breechloaders were employed in combat for the first time and, as the war went on, more and more muzzle-loaders were converted to breechloaders. The magazine-using repeating rifles that succeeded them became ancestors of the modern infantry rifle. Confederate armories, confronted with shortages of metals, machines, and craftsmen, made innovative use of substitutes but turned out some weapons with crudities.

The minié-ball, some examples of which are still being discovered by Civil War

"Old Rosy" — Union General William Rosecrans — dug in at Chattanooga after losing the Battle of Chickamauga. It took the combined efforts of Generals Grant, Sherman and Thomas to extricate him.

buffs equipped with metal detectors, had been adopted by the U.S. Army before the Civil War. It was an improved version of the bullet invented by Captain Claude Etienne Minié of France, which made loading a rifle as quick as loading a smoothbore. Self-contained cartridges, which would soon become standard, were invented during the war.

After the war, the United States Army adopted a breech-loading single-shot cartridge rifle as its standard weapon. The Hall rifle, the first breechloader adopted as a standard weapon by any nation, was also the first gun made in the United States to have fully interchangeable parts, an advantage that in time became a military necessity. The Hall carbine was the "first official U.S. gun manufactured as a percusion weapon."

The Brotherton House, past which the Confederate attack rolled in 1863 to rupture a Union center thrown off balance by the relocation of units, is as much a curiosity of life-style as a battlefield relic. The log cabin stands as it did then except that marble monuments and historical markers have replaced cattle in the yard and fields — and the nearby cannon are silent. While youngsters play on and around the can-

non, their parents poke their heads in at the cabin doorway to inspect the crude interior and spartan furnishings that were typical of the area during the period.

The cabin on Snodgrass Hill, whose site dominates the slope where thousands of Confederates fell trying to break the Union flank, has a bloodier history. Here, the stubborn stand earned Union General George H. Thomas the sobriquet "Rock of Chickamauga"; but the memorials remember the sacrifices of his troops, especially the 87th Indiana, 2nd Minnesota, and 9th Ohio Infantry Regiments. Thomas typified one kind of Federal soldier; a

Virginian by birth, he had elected to remain with the Union. He was a bold and imaginative leader who was even more aggressive than Grant — his troops pushed past their objective to capture Missionary Ridge at Chattanooga while Grant muttered threats of retribution if the action failed — and whose distinguished record led to command of the Army of the Cumberland.

The 1847 Gordon-Lee House, not far from the battlefield park, was used by the Federals first as a headquarters and then as a hospital. Behind its doric columns, rooms where generals huddled over maps

Union General George Thomas earned the nickname "Rock of Chickamauga" by holding fast against Confederate onslaughts in the vicinity of the Snodgrass Cabin.

The Lee and Gordon's Mill stood on Chickamauga Creek on one flank of the Union line. Confederate troops tried but failed to turn the Federal flank here on September 18, 1863.

A Confederate charge, led by General Longstreet, past the Brotherton House and across the farmland to strike the Union center, was the decisive action at Chickamauga.

and surgeons sawed off shattered arms and legs are now decorated with period furniture, Oriental floor coverings, and brass chandeliers.

Chickamauga would be the last Confederate chance to stop the Union invasion. When afterward Grant was made commander of all Union armies, in 1864, General William Tecumseh Sherman was put in charge of major military operations

Kolb's Farm, six miles south of Big Kennesaw Mountain and thus at one end of the battlefield park, was the first major clash of the two armies. The farmhouse, which General Joseph Hooker used as a Federal headquarters, has been restored to its mid-nineteenth-century appearance. The story of the June 22 attacks by Confederate General John B. Hood's corps is recounted there, where it happened, by a

in the west. He sent three armies — some 100,000 men — south from Chattanooga with the object of crushing the Confederate army of 50,000 under General Joseph E. Johnston and capturing Atlanta, a key rail hub and the "workhouse and warehouse of the South."

Bloody fighting — "Hell has broke loose in Georgia, sure enough," said one Confederate — would result at Kolb's Farm and Kennesaw Mountain, both of which are preserved in the Kennesaw Mountain National Battlefield Park; but the superior numbers of the Federals permitted Sherman to outflank Johnston on a number of occasions.

recorded message and exhibition on the trail leading away from the house. The fighting was inconclusive; the Confederates withdrew when night fell on their main line.

Five days later, Sherman launched a pair of coordinated attacks on Johnston's defenses. Trails and roads leading from the battlefield Visitors' Center to both Big Kennesaw Mountain and Cheatham's Hill cover the battle area, preserved earthworks, trenches, rifle pits, cannon, and exhibits explaining the progress of the fighting where it was "only necessary to expose a hand to procure a furlough." The best example of earthworks is at the top of

Cheatham Hill, where 8,000 Federal attackers suffered 1,580 casualties but could not dislodge the Confederates. Remains of the trenches they dug with bayonets and mess kits on hard-defended slopes may be seen below the Dead Angle, a Confederate salient where the bloodiest fighting of the battle took place. General Thomas, in command of the assault on the Confederate center, declared that "one or two more such assaults will use up this army." Unable to defeat Johnston by assault, Sherman resumed his flanking movement and Johnston had to withdraw.

The 10-minute slide presentation and exhibits at the Visitors' Center place the Kennesaw Mountain battle in the context of the struggle for Atlanta and the political climate in the North, where Abraham Lincoln's opponent in his run for a second

The Gordon-Lee House, which sheltered Union generals preparing for the Battle of Chickamauga, was built in 1847 by a Scottish immigrant who amassed a fortune in several businesses, including milling.

term in the presidency was General McClellan, the still-popular former commander of all the Union armies. Among the exhibits are paintings of the fighting and displays clarifying the functions of the various military branches, including the infantry — "the queen of battle" — which was so important at Kennesaw Mountain.

The *General*, the most famous locomotive in a war that demonstrated the strategic importance of railroads, is preserved at the Big Shanty Museum a few miles from Kennesaw Mountain battlefield. The great locomotive chase — used in this century as the subject of a Walt Disney movie — started only 100 yards from where the engine stands in the museum complex. Audio-visuals and other exhibits recreate the thrilling chase that

began when 22 Federal soldiers in civilian clothes, led by James Andrews, stole the engine while the passengers and crew were eating breakfast in the station at Kennesaw. The conductor, Captain William A. Fuller, and the crew doggedly pursued by foot, hand car, and commandeered engines, catching the raiders five miles from Chattanooga, their goal. Andrews and seven of his men were executed as spies.

Marietta and Roswell, north of Atlanta, were spared the destruction experienced by many places in Georgia. As a result, about 80 prewar buildings in Marietta and substantial numbers in Roswell and Madison reflect the traditions of the period. Among them are the 1855 Kennesaw House Hotel in Marietta, which Sherman used as a headquarters, captors of the

Hastily dug Union fortifications frame the lowlands of Kennesaw Mountain, Georgia, in 1864. Sherman decided to outflank the Confederate fortifications there after a costly attempt to take them.

General used as a conspiatorial meeting place, and which is now a restaurant; and in Roswell the Presbyterian church, which was pressed into service as a Federal hospital, and Barrington Hall. Lovejoy Plantation, built in 1838, was the inspiration for Twelve Oaks in *Gone With the Wind*.

Confederate officials, dissatisfied with Johnston's retrogression before Sherman's flanking movements, turned the defense of Atlanta over to General Hood. Hood launched savage attacks at Peachtree Creek, East Atlanta (this action is now known as the Battle of Atlanta), and Ezra Church within a period of eight days. Yet these moves did not prevent the occupation of Atlanta. The city became a burned-out hulk, and Sherman left to devastate a 60-mile-wide swath to the sea.

General William T. Sherman was given command in the Western Theater after Grant became Union general-in-chief.

Confederate General John Bell Hood conducted an aggressive defense of Atlanta, but was badly outnumbered.

Atlanta today has a unique combination of postwar recreations and genuine relics that escaped the fires. Grant Park — named for the donor of the land, not for the Union general — concentrates many of Atlanta's Civil War memories in a package convenient for the visitor. Remains of the city's fortifications, including Old Fort Walker and breastworks armed with old cannon, are complemented by the three-dimensional Cyclorama of the Battle of Atlanta. Narration, sound, and lighting effects recreate the battle of July 22, 1864, on a painting 50 feet high and 400 feet in circumference, which was completed in 1891. German and Polish artists oriented it to established landmarks and went out to the field to sketch the battle areas, so that the setting would be authentic down to the wooden bridges over dry washes and the raw earth of torn-up railroad tracks. Atlanta Municipal Park stands on part of the site of the Battle of Peachtree Creek, while Mozley Park preserves a small segment of the site of the Battle of Ezra Church.

The Confederate Memorial Carving at the Stone Mountain historical and entertainment complex a few miles east of Atlanta imposes huge equestrian figures of Jefferson Davis, Robert E. Lee, and Thomas J. "Stonewall" Jackson on the sheer northern face of an 825-foot-high granite dome measuring five miles around. The carving, which covers an area the size of a city block, is visible from most areas of the park and can be seen close at hand on a cable-car ride to the top of the rock. A feature of the "War in Georgia" exhibit at Confederate Hall is a relief map with lights, sound, and narration. Elsewhere in the park are a recreated antebellum plantation; a scenic railroad with replicas of the three steam engines used in the great railroad chase; a display on industries of the Old South; and a number of statues, including one of a mother holding a baby with the inscription, "The country comes before me", and another, of a soldier raising a broken sword, which bears the legend, "Men who saw night coming down on them could somehow act as if they stood on the edge of dawn."

While Sherman marched to the sea at Savannah, a Federal cavalry force moved into central Georgia from Alabama. Columbus fell; but an earthen fort at West Point held out all day on April 16, 1865. A water reservoir has been constructed on the site of the fort, but cemeteries off U.S.

This cannon stands on the strong hilltop position held by Confederates in the Battle of Kennesaw Mountain.

Peachtree Street (opposite bottom), Atlanta's main thoroughfare, was not impressive as shown here in 1864, but the city was an industrial center as well as a railroad hub.

Destruction of the railroad tracks near Atlanta was only a sample of the devastation that followed. General Hood's wrecked ammunition train is shown below here.

Route 29 and in LaGrange hold the graves of nearly 400 Confederate and Union soldiers. The Griggs House, from which Northern sharpshooters fired into the fort, retains much of its 1865 appearance; it is a private residence.

Columbus, an inland port on the Chattahoochee River, is the home of the Confederate Naval Museum, where salvaged remains of the gunboat C.S.S. *Chattahoochee* and ironclad ram C.S.S. *Jackson* can be seen. The Infantry Museum at nearby Fort Benning has a Medal of Honor Room and Civil War mementoes among its collection. Fitzgerald has a Civil War connection unique among Georgia cities: It was founded as a colony of Union soldiers who remained behind after the war.

The last session of the Confederate Congress was held in Macon's City Hall, which had been built as a bank in 1835 but was acquired by the state during the war. Among other antebellum structures in the city is one known as the Old Cannonball House because it was struck during a Federal attack in 1864. Bibb County casualties are remembered by the Confederate Monument. At the 1855 Bellevue mansion in LaGrange, the owner and members of the Confederate Cabinet surrendered in April 1865; the house is open to the public.

Remnants of Atlanta's strong defensive works, this one armed with a Napoleon gun (foreground), may still be seen.

Railroad facilities, such as this ruined engine house and trains without tracks on which to move, were a primary objective of the Union attack on Atlanta.

A prisoner-of-war camp, named Fort Sumter by the Confederacy but better known by the name of Andersonville, the railroad stop where the prisoners arrived, is 10 miles northeast of Americus on Georgia Route 49. It recalls one of the great tragedies of the war. Constructed to provide better conditions for Federal prisoners, it became instead a hell-hole for those who were sent there because of overcrowding, inadequate facilities and supplies, and the preying of some prisoners on others.

Andersonville National Historic Site preserves some of the features, including the spring that became so polluted that freshness caused by rain inspired the prisoners to name it Providence Spring; earthworks and rifle pits that were part of the fortifications; and holes dug as escape tunnels and in attempts to find water. Memorials honor the soldiers who died there, some individuals, and the Women's Relief Corps, an auxiliary of the Grand Army of the Republic that operated the site until it was turned over to the U.S. government in 1910. The more than 12,000 men who died there are buried in the national cemetery. Among them are six "Andersonville raiders," ringleaders of the group of prisoners who preyed on their fellows until caught and executed on July 11, 1864. The commandant of the camp, Captain Henry Wirz, was tried by a

Crowded conditions made the prison camp at Andersonville, Georgia, officially known as Camp Sumter, a hell-hole for Union prisoners of war. They also suffered from inadequate housing, food, and medical attention in the last days of the war, when supplies were scarce in the Confederacy. The prisoners built wooden huts, called "shebangs," for shelter.

*Prisoners who died at
Andersonville were buried
in long trenches, as this
photo from 1864 shows.*

Federal military tribunal after the war and hanged in Washington, D.C.

The town of Andersonville now has a welcome center and museum, as well as a country farm in a five-acre park.

The 176-foot-high brick chimney, all that remains of the South's principal gunpowder factory, and the Arsenal, now part of a college, recall Augusta's primary role in the Civil War. The First Presbyterian Church was used for a time as a hospital and temporary detention camp. Lieu-

Wooden headboards, used initially to identify the more than 12,000 prisoners who died at Andersonville, have been replaced by permanent markers and small flags. The dove on the headstone below is an unusual feature.

tenant General Leonidas K. Polk, nick-named "the fighting bishop of the Confederacy," is entombed in a crypt beneath the altar of St. Paul's Episcopal Church. Augusta was spared Sherman's torch, it is said, because he had once fallen in love with an Augustan girl, the sister of his West Point roommate.

Sherman's famous March to the Sea ended at Savannah, which surrendered so as to avoid destruction and thus retains much of its original appearance. This includes the orderly squares mapped out by General James Edward Oglethorpe in the 1730s and numerous early–nineteenth-century houses that witnessed the Civil War. Factor's Walk (restored) particularly reflects the lively commercial life of the Confederate port and navy yard.

Savannah's martial aspect is its four forts. Fort Pulaski, described as being "as strong as the Rocky Mountains" when completed in 1847, still bears the scars of the 30-hour Federal bombardment on April 10–11, 1864, which demonstrated to the world the destructive power of the new rifled cannon: When the Confederates were forced to surrender, the era of brick citadels was over.

Artillery for the attack was hauled ashore at Tybee Island, where the museum now occupying one of the gun batteries of post–Civil War Fort Screven has a Civil War room emphasizing documents, artifacts, and memorabilia of Sherman's arrival at Savannah. Museum displays and living-history demonstrations at Fort Jackson, built in the early 1800s but

Sherman completed his march to the sea in 1864 by entering Savannah, Georgia, which the Confederates evacuated rather than defend.

Fort Pulaski was part of the ring of fortifications defending Savannah. Union use of rifled cannon, the effects of which still show on some of the brick walls, forever changed the way forts are built.

substantially altered after the Civil War, relive the fort's history, including the Civil War period, when it was headquarters for the batteries defending the river approaches to Savannah. Part of the earthworks and battery site erected at Wormsloe Plantation, whose 1744 tabby house stands about eight miles southeast of the city, are still visible.

Fort MacAllister, an earthworks fort 10 miles east of Richmond Hill on U.S. Route 17, successfully resisted attacks by monitor-type Union warships, demonstrating once again that earthen fortifications could survive the heaviest naval bombardment possible at the time. Its 220 defenders finally succumbed to an attack by an entire division of Sherman's army in December of 1864, making the fall of Savannah inevitable.

(Overleaf) Stone Mountain, near Atlanta, is the world's largest granite monolith. It is the centerpiece of an historical and entertainment complex. A city-block — sized sculpture (inset) on the face of the 825-foot-high mountain features equestrian statues of Lee, Jackson and Davis.

WESTERN TERRITORIES & STATES

The western territories and states were as diverse as any part of the nation, but were to a large extent isolated from what was generally referred to as The East. Settlers of the organized territories and the few states already admitted to the Union had come from both warring regions and tended to divide loyalties along lines of origin. The Civil War reached out to touch them all in significant and sometimes poignant ways, and thus was as much a national as a sectional war.

The Confederacy coveted the southwest, both as a way of extending slavery and as a source of precious metals to help finance a war that strained the finances of an agricultural region. Unionists were determined to keep their areas under the national government, and Republicans recognized the opportunity to strengthen and entrench their party in California, where the decade of the 1850s had produced a strong independence movement, and in the territories that later would become states. For many Indians, a war between the whites provided an opportunity to regain control of their own lands and destinies.

Such unstable conditions invited tragedy, and it came quickly. Kansas, which had been settled by organized, competitive immigration efforts from New England and the mid-South during the 1850s, miraculously escaped most of the fighting between Confederate and Federal armies, although the Battle of Mine Creek occurred as an aftermath of Confederate General Sterling Price's gamble at Westport, Missouri. Kansas continued to bleed from the marauding attacks of irregulars throughout the war, with the 1863 raid on Lawrence becoming a symbol of depravity, and was affected by the hostilities initiated by the Indians seeking to take advantage of the Civil War.

Kansas

Although Kansas received many of the wounds of the Civil War, it has few of the scars. Fort Scott, a frontier sanctuary (still well preserved today), was reopened as a Union supply depot near the Missouri-Kansas border. It may well have been the target Confederate units retreating from Missouri after the Battle of Westport in October, 1864 were heading for until Union forces caught up with them at Mine Creek, north of the town. Fort Leavenworth was a Union stronghold, too, and the museum on this still-active military post owns the carriage that President Abraham Lincoln used on a visit to the fort and exhibits a good collection of military uniforms up through World War II. An audio-visual slide show telling the history of the fort is shown on a regular schedule. At Manhattan, the Beecher Bible and Rifle Church recalls the practice of

Beecher Bible and Rifle Church in Kansas got its name from crates marked "Bibles," which actually contained weapons for antislavery forces.

using crates marked "Bibles" to import arms bought with money donated by the Rev. Henry Ward Beecher's congregation in Brooklyn, New York.

A rest stop on U.S. Route 69 south of Pleasanton marks the site of the Battle of Mine Creek, largest formal battle in Kansas. Although 228 acres of the battlefield are preserved, there are few amenities for visitors. Points of interest are marked on two self-guided trails, and an historical marker at the highway turnout relates the highlights of the battle, which occurred October 25, 1864, when Confederate troops hastily formed positions to blunt Union pursuit. The Union attack drove many into the nearby creek bottom, where they were captured after heavy hand-to-hand combat; but the Union pursuit was stopped and General Price was able to continue his retreat. More than 25,000 men were involved in the battle, more than in any other engagement on Kansas soil.

The final leg of Price's retreat, which took him through the rugged and inhospitable Indian Territory, was harder on his army than the Battle of Mine Creek, but his exhausted forces finally reached their base in Arkansas.

The Brown family of Kansas was notorious — or famous, depending on the point of view — as abolitionists long before John went east to capture the arsenal at Harper's Ferry. In 1856, after the Browns and their followers had attacked the homes of proslavery farmers and killed several of them, proslavery supporters retaliated with a raid that became known as the Battle of Osawatomie. Irregular fighting of this kind was intensified by the outbreak of formal war, and devastated Kansas throughout the Civil War. Union attempts to halt the attacks even extended to the point of arresting the female relatives of Confederate irregulars and jailing them at Kansas City, Missouri. The deaths of some of them in an accident contributed to one of the most famous raids of the war, the destruction of Lawrence, an antislavery stronghold, in 1863.

While William Clark Quantrill promoted the raid as a way to redress the Confederate defeat at Gettysburg, some of his lieutenants were persuaded to go along because of the accident in Kansas City. The 450 raiders were in no mood to be lenient, and Quantrill had given orders to kill all the men and burn every house. This order was sytematically carried out in a house-to-house search for valuables and horses. No women were harmed, according to the Bushwhackers code, and a few men survived by hiding out in various ways. Among them was James Henry

S. J. R. del. 24. 06

*The only major battle
fought in Kansas, at Mine
Creek, is depicted in this
contemporary sketch.
Confederates halted there
to blunt pursuit after losing
the Battle of Westport in
Missouri.*

Lane, a puzzling politician who was himself a proficient leader of Union raids. In 1861, he had taken delight in destroying Missouri towns that had welcomed the Confederate units victorious at Lexington. His cavalry fired indiscriminately on a charge through Osceola, then set fire to almost all the buildings after finding a cache of lead, powder, and cartridge paper. His men had a more personally satisfying way of destroying barrels of brandy, 3,000 sacks of flour, 500 pounds of sugar and molasses, 50 sacks of coffee, and a quantity of bacon.

Lawrence is more famous today for a role that had been selected before the Civil War — as the site of the University of Kansas. A number of historic buildings remain in the downtown area and the Old West Lawrence Historic District.

Indian Territories
Both North and South were accused of fomenting Indian uprisings, but neither government condoned such action, nor did regular forces in the field encourage Indian violence. However, the sight of whites fighting each other was a psychological

One of Kansas' most feared raiders, William C. Quantrill, sacked Lawrence to redress the Confederate defeat at Gettysburg.

James H. Lane, a puzzling politician and Union raider, survived the destruction of Lawrence by hiding out.

stimulant, and the Civil War divided many Indian tribes in much the same manner as it split white families and clans in the border states. Many saw the division of the white men as an opportunity to reverse the invasion of settlers and opportunists, and periodic uprisings troubled both frontiersmen and the contesting armies. Others counseled peace as a means of retaining the economic gains they had made under a sedentary way of life. Many well-to-do Indians owned slaves. Both the Confederates and the Federals recruited Indian soldiers into their regular forces.

Indian conflict was periodic, but it ranged all the way from Minnesota to the New Mexico Territory and even involved the Five Civilized Tribes in Indian Territory, now the state of Oklahoma. There were small, intense battles that were only vaguely related to the Civil War and more properly should be regarded as portents of the fitful warring that would persist almost to the end of the century as Indian resistance to continually increasing settlement mounted. A number of them are included in tabulations of Civil War battles, however, although few of the sites have been developed to receive visitors.

The most destructive Indian uprising during the Civil War — certainly, the one most publicized in the press — was that of the Sioux nation in Minnesota in August of 1862. The tribe has signed away its lands in eastern Minnesota in 1851 in exchange for annual payments and a guaranteed million acres reserved to their use, but many of the tribe members had been unhappy with the arrangement, and the payments were frequently late. Traders took advantage of the financial naïveté of the Indians to keep them in debt, and some of these debt claims were simply fraudulent. These nomadic Indians also resented white attempts to Christianize them and to turn them into farmers.

The situation was ripe for violence, but it did not actually begin until some young braves taunted another, saying he was afraid of white men. To show his peers that he wasn't, he shot a farmer near Acton, and his taunters followed up by killing four others, including a woman and a girl. They fled to the reservation, where their story divided the tribe into two groups, one wanting to surrender the braves and take the consequences and the other willing to take the warpath. The Indians, apparently following a preconceived plan of driving all whites back across the Mississippi River, attacked some well-defended areas, including Fort Ridgely and New Ulm, where at least a third of the town was destroyed. Some Winnebagos joined the uprising, producing fear of a general Indian insurrection — which did not materialize. However, the Sioux rampage was one of the worst massacres in American history, killing at least 800 and driving thousands from their farms and settlements to the safety of St. Paul and Fort Ridgely.

New Ulm preserves a number of relics from the period, including the Frederick W. Kiesling building on North Minesota Street (now the offices of the Chamber of Commerce); it was filled with hay so that it could be burned to provide light for defense, if needed. Women and children took refuge in the Frank Erd building (part of the original remains). The Frederick Forster building — which, along with the Henry Schalk building, was a principal defense point during the uprising — has been altered but retains original features. The ruins of the Wajaru Distillery and displays and paintings in the Brown County Historical Museum, together with the Defenders' Monument, erected by the state of Minnesota in 1891, also recall the heroic defense of the town by its citizens. Fort Ridgely, about 20 miles from New Ulm, has been partly restored and has an interpretive center for the visitor.

Although the area north of the Minnesota River was most affected, the side effects extended beyond the Iowa border and into the Dakota Territory. The uprising was broken by a campaign conducted by Brigadier General Henry Hastings Sibley, a former governor, who had lived and traded with the Sioux for 28 years and knew them well.

The Battle of Wood Lake on September 23, 1862, was actually an Indian ambush that was accidentally discovered. It raged for two hours and included close combat. The rout of 500 braves there strengthened the hand of the Indians who had opposed the war path from the start, and the warring faction began to dwindle as Sibley pushed up the Minnesota River Valley. War parties continued to operate under Little Crow, the nominal leader of the uprising; but gradually the Indians returned to the reservation.

Little Crow was soon after killed in the fighting, but 306 other leaders were convicted and given the death penalty. President Lincoln, noting that the evidence against most of them was unconvincing, commuted the sentences of all but 38; those were hanged in a mass execution at Mankato on December 26, 1862.

In the Indian Territory, three battles indicate the bitterness of the divisions among the Indians. Creeks under Chief Opothleyoholo would not support the Confederacy, as most of their tribesmen did, and began a pilgrimage to Kansas, where they thought they would be safe. Superior Indian and Texas units caught up with them on November 19, 1861, but were repulsed in the confusing night Battle of Round Mounds. The next morning, Opothleyoholo and his band were gone; but later they were discovered at Bird Creek by a mixed-blood named Clem Rogers, the father of humorist Will Rogers. This battle ended in a draw, with the pursuing force returning to Fort Gibson. The fleeing band was attacked again at Shoal Creek, however, and broken into smaller units, which were hunted down.

New Mexico Territory

At the outbreak of the Civil War, the New Mexico Territory (now the states of New

Fort Larned was one of the frontier forts which protected Kansas from both partisans and Indians.

Mexico and Arizona) was a sparsely settled, lightly defended area with considerable appeal for the Confederacy. It extended almost to the West Coast, had sizable stocks of weapons and supplies stored at Federal forts, and was the gateway to great mineral wealth, both inside and outside its boundaries. Texans invaded the territory soon after the war began and precipitated a showdown that involved maneuver as much as fighting, but which from time to time produced spirited battles between the small forces involved.

At first, Confederates met with success against small Union forces divided among a number of posts. Mesilla was proclaimed capital of the Confederate territory after the surrender of Fort Fillmore to Colonel John Baylor.

Union defenders traded land for time and concentration of forces, surrendering forts and towns in the southern part of the territory almost without a fight as 3,700 Confederates advanced northward along the banks of the Rio Grande River.

The first major conflict occurred on February 21, 1862, at Valverde, about six miles north of Fort Craig and three miles east of the present U.S. Route 85 a hundred miles south of Albuquerque. The invading Confederates threatened the fort's supply lines. Union troops sent to keep the Confederates from crossing the river drove them back, and gradually the forces of both sides were committed piecemeal as the fighting continued. One feature of the battle was "one of the most gallant and furious charges ... ever witnessed in the annals of battles" by Texas lancers — Confederates on the frontier were armed with whatever weapons were available. They were beaten back with heavy losses. In the end, the battle was decided by a furious Confederate charge against the artillery on one Union flank. Colonel Edward R.S. Canby, who commanded the Union forces, pulled his men back to the fort, leaving the guns behind.

The ratio of casualties to the number of men involved was high on both sides, but the Confederate victory produced sizable stores of small arms and supplies, in addition to the captured cannon. A truce was declared for two days while both armies treated their wounded and buried their dead, after which Colonel Canby again refused to surrender the fort. The Confederate commander, Brigadier General Sibley, then bypassed the fort and marched on to capture Albuquerque and Santa Fe. Neither the battlefield nor ruins of the fort is accessible to the public.

The most significant Civil War battle in the New Mexico Territory, sometimes called the Gettysburg of the West, is reenacted each year at Pigeon's Ranch, 19 miles southeast of Santa Fe, by history organizations — in 1984, 120 uniformed youth represented the principal Texas and Colorado units and the United States regulars involved in the Battle of Glorietta.

Army records list two battles, but the first encounter on March 26, 1862, at Apache Canyon was only a preliminary to the combat at Glorietta Pass two days later. The site of the latter is preserved, but only partly developed for visitors. The ruins of a three-room adobe ranch structure remain to mark the site where Confederate and Union forces struggled in furious hand-to-hand battle over rugged terrain. Although Union forces retreated to their base at the Kozlowski Ranch after the battle, the Confederates could not pursue because their supply train had been destroyed by a cavalry detachment led by Major John M. Chivington.

Fort Union, the principal Federal bastion against the Confederate invasion, was untouched. At Fort Union National Monument, a self-guided 1.25-mile trail leads to adobe and brick ruins; the Visitors' Center highlights the history of three successive forts to protect the region from 1851 to 1891, including undeveloped remains of the Civil War earthen fort. Those who fell in the New Mexico battles are buried in the Santa Fe National Cemetery.

The loss of their supplies and ammunition at Glorietta Pass forced the Confederates to retreat to Santa Fe, and then to their base at Albuquerque. As more Federal reinforcements arrived from Colorado, and the California Column moved from southern California into the southern part of the territory, Sibley abandoned Albuquerque and, after an indecisive battle at Peralta, retreated to his base at Fort Bliss, Texas.

The Confederate threat to the territory was effectively over, but the fighting was just beginning for the California and Colorado Volunteers. Warfare with the Indians of the region was frequent; it became so savage that men who lamented having to destroy horses they could not take with them willingly killed Indians. Log forts continued to sprout along the established trails in an effort to protect settlers and

Hardly noticed in the East, the Battle of Glorietta Pass, New Mexico, blocked the Confederate invasion of the southwestern territories. This re-enactment is an annual event.

traders, but the campaigns conducted by Colonel Christopher "Kit" Carson were more effective in forcing the Indians onto the Bosque Redondos Reservation.

Carson's campaign against the Apaches in 1862 and the Navahos in 1863 – 64 were typical. His tactic was to maintain pressure by a series of encircling maneuvers that resulted in small engagements and kept those nations from uniting. Canyon de Chelly National Monument near Gallup, New Mexico, preserves the Navaho stronghold Carson invaded in an effort to break their resistance. Indian guides now lead visitors through the rugged 35-mile-long canyon, whose walls rise 1,000 feet in places. An attempt to arrest Cochise and his followers resulted in a substantial fight on July 16, 1862, between the Apaches and a detachment of California Volunteers. It was a Hollywood-style battle, with the Apaches attacking and withdrawing, then ambushing the soldiers from the high ground in the pass. The Apaches lost, and were permanently denied one of their favorite haunts by the erection of Fort Bowie, which continued active until 1894.

The flag in the plaza at Taos flies 24 hours a day because of an incident that occurred during the Civil War. Carson had the Stars and Stripes nailed to the flagpole and set a guard to prevent it from being taken down. The Kit Carson Museum, a half-block from the plaza, retains numerous mementoes of the famous Indian fighter.

Present-day Arizona lays claim to the "westernmost battle" of the Civil War. On April 15, 1862, units of the California Column encountered a 16-man Confederate raiding detachment at Picacho Pass near the Santa Cruz River, now far from the main highways. Most of the Texans escaped, and presumably returned to the Confederate base at Tucson.

California

California might have been the first state to secede — to form the Pacific Republic — if separatist sentiment in the early 1850s had won. The Civil War renewed the argument between Unionists and separatists, and resulted in both tragic and comical situations. Southern California expressed strongly pro-Confederate sympathies, and even in San Francisco loyalty rallies were required to sustain support for the Union government far away in

Washington; Union Square gets its name from being used for those rallies. Secret societies favorable to the Confederacy existed everywhere, some resulting in unsuccessful plots like the one to take over the navy yard as a preliminary to capturing San Francisco.

No battles between Union and Confederate forces were fought in California, but the state remained jittery throughout the war and experienced numerous rumors of the approach of Confederate raiding vessels and the rising up of Confederate sympathizers. Southern sympathizers traveled eastward through the New Mexico Territory to enroll in the Confederate cause. One of the principal functions of troops stationed in southern California

was to block this trickle of resources for the Confederacy.

In San Francisco, Fort Point, now a national historical park with a 30-minute guided tour and cannon demonstrations, was kept in turmoil by rumors of Confederate invasions of San Francisco Bay and by the demands of the Unionist population. The role of Alcatraz as the other principal bastion guarding the harbor has been overshadowed in modern times by its later service as a prison.

Actually, Indians were a greater problem than Confederates. A dozen skirmishes along the Eel River north of San Francisco are listed as Civil War actions but really were part of the growing resentment of the Indians against white en-

Fort Point, at the entrance to San Francisco harbor, stood alone when it was built in 1861, but now is dominated by the Golden Gate bridge.

San Francisco teemed with rumors of Southern invasions and local insurgency plots, but life at Fort Mason and other fortifications was dull, as the bullet holes left by bored soldiers testify.

croachment. To the south, turning Catalina Island into an Indian reservation was one solution that got serious consideration. In fact, the island was occupied by Federal troops, who removed all nonessential civilians, in preparation for that use, before the idea was rejected in Washington.

Texas

Texas escaped heavy fighting during the Civil War largely because of geography; but the state was a major contributor to the Confederate cause. Until the Mississippi was closed by Federal troops and gunboats, Texas was a major source of supplies and manpower. Texans fought on all fronts, from Virginia to Arizona, and saved many a battle by their stalwartness. Colonel Taylor, from his base at Mesilla, redrew the map of the New Mexico Territory as a Confederate territory, with Arizona as a separate jurisdiction. General Sibley's grueling invasion of New Mexico along the Rio Grande moved from his base in San Antonio through El Paso. At home, Indians were a greater problem than Federal forces. Texas units occupied Forts

Washita, Cobb, and Arbuckle in an unsuccessful attempt to secure the northern part of the state against Indian attacks. Home Guard units were entrusted with internal protection and succeeded in keeping the Indians relatively quiet until 1865. At the Battle of Dove Creek on January 8, 1865, guardsmen reinforced by some regulars defeated a band of Indians.

In Austin, the state capital, there is a historical museum jointly maintained by the Daughters of the Confederacy and the Daughters of the Republic of Texas. Placita Santa Fe, El Paso's Old Town, retains the adobe and stone buildings that were standard when Sibley and his troops passed through. Hillsboro's Confederate Research Center and Audie Murphy Gun Museum has a sizable collection of Civil War relics, including photographs and weapons. The Fort Bend County Museum at Richmond displays local Civil War mementoes. Prisoner-of-war camps were located at Camp Groce on the Brazos River near Hempstead and at Camp Ford near Tyler.

Federal attacks on Texas were concen-

Colonel "Kit" Carson (opposite) invaded the rugged but beautiful Canyon de Chelly in New Mexico, a Navaho stronghold, to keep the Indians from taking advantage of the Civil War.

trated on the coast. Galveston was captured by the Union late in 1862, but it was retaken on January 1, 1863, by Confederate General John B. Magruder. Galveston's subsequent bouts with hurricanes have left few relics of its Civil War history, but the city retains the flavor of the economic freebooting that began when the pirate Jean Lafitte made it his headquarters. It cherishes its historic buildings — especially the Williams Home and the Ashton Villa, which date from before the war — and its Gulf Coast personality, protected by its long massive seawall.

The only sizable battle between Con-

federate and Union regulars in Texas was an unqualified success for the Confederates. On September 8, 1863, a combined Federal army and navy force assembled by General Nathaniel P. Banks and Admiral David G. Farragut launched an invasion of the state at Sabine Pass. Nowadays, a pretty state park overlooking the pass preserves the site of the battlefield where several hundred Confederates under Lieutenant Richard Dowling drove the 4,000-man invasion force back to their ships. Naturally, Dowling became a great hero to the Texans.

Two months later General Banks in-

The tension between Northern and Southern sympathizers in San Francisco may have been one reason Federal commanders stored tons of ammunition on Alcatraz Island in the bay.

Alcatraz Island, better known for its later role as a prison, was fortified to protect San Francisco Bay during the Civil War.

vaded the Rio Grande Valley and captured Brownsville and nearby points (November 1863), then pushed up the coast to occupy Mustang Island, off Corpus Christi, and Fort Esperanza, on Matagorda Island. The following summer the Confederates liberated Brownsville, but they were not able to reopen the Rio Grande to traffic. Historic buildings of Fort Brown — better remembered for its use in the Mexican War — are now incorporated into a junior college. The port, through which goods from abroad reached the Confederacy until 1863, now harbors a large fishing fleet and is an outlet for the citrus products of the river valley.

Intemperate acts occurred in Texas, as they did elsewhere, because of the passions that divided the people. German settlers, who were outspoken in their opposition to slavery and firm in allegiance to the Union, were attacked on August 10, 1862, by a Confederate ranger force. Casualties in the Battle of Neuces, as the engagement is called, were not large, but the numbers grew as clashes between Confederates and Unionists continued. Gainesville, in Gilespie County, not far from the Oklahoma border, was the setting for the Great Hanging in which a Texas ranger, Captain

The U.S.S. Camanche *was the first assemble-it-yourself warship. Dismantled and shipped to the West Coast in the hold of a cargo vessel to counter threats of Confederate raiders — real and fancied — it was reassembled in San Francisco by Peter Donahue. The Passaic-class ironclad monitor, shown here in 1864 during reassembly, was not commissioned until 1865.*

James Duff, hanged about 50 men and killed a number of others.

Texas was the last holdout as the Civil War wound down, and the final battle of the "cruel war" was fought at Palmito Ranch, east of Brownsville, on May 12, 1865 — a month after Lee had surrendered at Appomattox.

Although Lee's decision was soundly denounced, the inevitability of surrender brought political leaders of Texas, Arkansas, Louisiana, and Missouri to a meeting in Marshall with General E. Kirby Smith to draft a capitulation agreement. When a few of Smith's officers threatened to arrest him unless he continued the war, he turned the command over to Lieutenant General Simon Bolivar Buckner, who went to New Orleans amd surrendered his command on paper. Some of Buckner's officers complied — and some did not. General Stand Watie was probably the last Confederate to surrender his forces formally — on June 23, 1865. Others, including Colonel Jo Shelby, emigrated — some only briefly and others permanently — to Mexico, California, British Honduras, and Brazil.

Some things had been settled and some had not. The Union was preserved, but the bitterness caused by the war and Reconstruction would become part of the psyche of the nation. So would the mystique of The Cause in the South. The contest between state's rights and federalism was not resolved; it exists today.

DIRECTORY
OF BATTLEFIELDS AND RELATED SITES

Visiting hours can vary with the season at many battlefield parks and related sites. It's a good idea to check ahead. All sites are happy to provide brochures and other information for those planning visits.

ALABAMA

Burritt Museum
US Route 431
Huntsville, AL 35804

Civil War Museum
Fort Gaines
Dauphin Island, AL 36528

First White House of the
   Confederacy
Hall St.
Montgomery, AL 36104

Fort Morgan
Gulf Shores Peninsula
Mobile Point, AL 36542

ARIZONA

Canyon de Chelly National
   Monument
Box 588
Chinle, AZ 86503

ARKANSAS

Arkansas Post National Memorial
Route 1, Box 16
Gillett, AR 72055

Pea Ridge National Military Park
US Route 62
Pea Ridge, AR 72751

Prairie Grove Battlefield State Park
US Route 62
Prairie Grove, AR 72753

CALIFORNIA

Fort Point National Historic Site
Box 29333
Presidio of San Francisco, CA 94129

Golden Gate National Recreation
   Area
Fort Mason
San Francisco, CA 94123

FLORIDA

Fort Jefferson National Monument
c/o US Coast Guard Base
Key West, FL 33040

Fort Pickens
Gulf Islands National Seashore
Box 100
Gulf Breeze, FL 32561

Natural Bridge State Historic Site
State Route 363
Woodville, FL 32362

Olustee Battlefield Historic
   Memorial
US Route 90
Olustee, FL 32072

GEORGIA

Andersonville National Historic Site
Andersonville, GA 31711

Chickamauga and Chattanooga
   National Military Park
Box 2126
Fort Oglethorpe, GA 30742

Confederate Naval Museum
Columbus, GA 31902

Fort Pulaski National Monument
Box 98
Tybee Island, GA 31328

Kennesaw Mountain National
   Battlefield Park
Box 1167
Marietta, GA 30061

KANSAS

Fort Larned National Historic Site
Route 3
Fort Larned, KS 67550

Fort Scott National Historic Site
Old Fort Blvd.
Fort Scott, KS 66701

KENTUCKY

Abraham Lincoln Birthplace
   National Historic Site
RFD 1
Hodgenville, KY 42748

Columbus-Belmont Battlefield State
   Park
Columbus, KY 42032

Cumberland Gap National
   Historical Park
Box 840
Middlesboro, KY 40965

Jefferson Davis Monument State
   Park
Fairview, KY 42221

Perryville Battlefield State Shrine
Box 231
Perryville, KY 40468

LOUISIANA

Camp Moore State Commemorative
   Area
State Route 51 north of
Amite, LA
Box 15
Tangipahoar, LA 70465

Confederate Museum
929 Camp St.
New Orleans, LA 70130

Fort Pike State Commemorative
   Area
US Route 90
Malheureux Point, LA

Mansfield State Commemorative
   Area
State Route 175 south of
Mansfield, LA 71052

Port Hudson State Commemorative
 Area
US Route 61 north of
Baton Rouge
Box 453
Zachary, LA 70791

MARYLAND

Antietam National Battlefield
Box 158
Sharpsburg, MD 21782

Clara Barton National Historic Site
5801 Oxford Rd.
Glen Echo, MD 20768

Point Lookout State Park
State Route 5
Point Lookout, MD

MISSISSIPPI

Beauvoir Mansion
Box 200
Biloxi, MS 39531

Brices Cross Roads National
 Battlefield Site
c/o Natchez Trace Parkway
RR 1, NT-143
Tupelo, MS 38801

The Curlee House
301 Childs St.
Corinth, MS 38834

Grand Gulf Military Park
Route 2, Box 389
Port Gibson, MS 39150

Ship Island
Gulf Islands National Seashore
Box T
Ocean Springs, MS 39564

Tupelo National Battlefield
c/o Natchez Trace Parkway
RR1, NT-143
Tupelo, MS 38801

Vicksburg National Military Park
Box 349
Vicksburg, MS 39180

MISSOURI

Battle of Lexington State Historic
 Site
US Route 24
Lexington, MO 64067

Bushwhacker Museum
Nevada, MO 64772

Confederate Memorial State Park
State Routes 13 and 20
Higginsville, MO 64037

Fort Davidson State Historical Park
State Route 21
Ironton, MO 63650

New Madrid Historical Museum
New Madrid, MO 63869

Wilson's Creek National Battlefield
Route 2, Box 75
Republic, MO 65738

NEW MEXICO

Kit Carson Museum
Taos, NM 87571

Fort Union National Monument
Watrous, NM 87753

NORTH CAROLINA

Bennett Place State Historical Park
US Route 70
Durham, NC 27705

Bentonville Battlefield
State Route 18 near
Newton Grove, NC 28366

Fort Anderson
Brunswick Town State Historic Site
Box 356
Southport, NC 28461

Fort Raleigh National Historic Site
c/o Cape Hatteras National
 Seashore
Route 1, Box 675
Manteo, NC 28731

PENNSYLVANIA

Gettysburg National Military Park
Gettysburg, PA 17325

SOUTH CAROLINA

Fort Sumter National Monument
1214 Middle St.
Sullivans Island, SC 29482

TENNESSEE

Britton's Lane Battlefield
Denmark, TN 38391

Sam Davis Birthplace
US Route 70
Smyrna, TN 37167

Nathan Bedford Forrest Memorial
 Park
Camden, TN 38320

Fort Donelson National Military
 Park
PO Box F
Dover, TN 37058

Fort Pillow State Historic Area
Henning, TN 38041

Hale Springs Inn
Rogersville, TN 37857

Lookout Mountain. *See*
Chickamauga and Chattanooga
 National Military Park, Georgia.

Andrew Johnson National Historic
 Site
Depot St.
Greeneville, TN 37743

Shiloh National Military Park
Shiloh, TN 38376

Stones River National Battlefield
Route 10, Box 401
Old Nashville Highway
Murfreesboro, TN 37130

WEST VIRGINIA

Carnifax Ferry Battlefield
State Route 39
Keslers Cross Lanes, WV 26675

Droop Mountain Battlefield
US Route 219
Droop, WV 24933

Harpers Ferry National Historical
    Park
PO Box 65
Harpers Ferry, WV 25425

VIRGINIA

Appomattox Court House National
    Historic Park
PO Box 218
Appomattox, VA 24522

Arlington House, The Robert E. Lee
    Memorial
c/o George Washington Memorial
    Parkway
Turkey Run Park
McLean, VA 22101

Battle Abbey
Boulevard and Kensington Aves.
Richmond, VA 23221

Belle Grove Plantation
US Route 11
Middletown, VA 22645

Berkeley Plantation
Route 5
Charles City, VA 23030

Blandford Church and Cemetery
319 S. Crater Rd.
Petersburg, VA 23803

Boyhood Home of Robert E. Lee
607 Oronoco St.
Alexandria, VA 22313

Casemate Museum
Bernard Road
Hampton, VA 23351

Colonial National Historic Park
Yorktown National Cemetery
Box 210
Yorktown, VA 23690

The Culpeper Cavalry Museum
133 W. Davis St.
Culpeper, VA 22701

Fort Monroe
Old Point Comfort
E. Mercury Blvd.
Hampton, VA 23351

Fredericksburg and Spotsylvania
    County Battlefields Memorial
    National Military Park
Box 679
Fredericksburg, VA 22401

Fort Ward Museum and Historic
    Site
4301 West Braddock Rd.
Alexandria, VA 22313

Hollywood Cemetery
Cherry and Albermarle St.
Richmond, VA 23219

Stonewall Jackson's Headquarters
415 N. Braddock St.
Winchester, VA 22601

Stonewall Jackson House
8 E. Washington St.
Lexington, VA 24450

Stonewall Jackson's Grave
Main St.
Lexington, VA 24450

Stonewall Jackson Shrine
Route 606
Guinea, VA

Lee Chapel
Washington and Lee University
Lexington, VA 24450

Manassas National Battlefield Park
PO Box 350
Manassas, VA 22110

Museum of the Confederacy
12th and Clay Sts.
Richmond, VA 23219

New Market Battlefield Park and
    Hall of Valor
Route I-81
New Market, VA 22844

Petersburg National Battlefield
Box 549
Petersburg, VA 23803

Petersburg Siege Museum
Bank St.
Petersburg, VA 23803

Richmond National Battlefield Park
3215 East Broad St.
Richmond, VA 23223

The Robert E. Lee House
707 E. Franklin St.
Richmond, VA 23223

Sayler's Creek Battlefield Historical
    State Park
State Route 617
Rice, VA 23966

Spotsylvania Court House
    Battlefield
Box 679
Route 208
Spotsylvania, VA 22553

Warren Rifles Confederate Museum
Chester St.
Front Royal, VA 22630

The White House of the
    Confederacy
12th and Clay Sts.
Richmond, VA 23223

Wilderness Battlefield
Route 3
Fredericksburg, VA 22401

INDEX

Numbers in italics indicate illustrations.

Illustration Credits

Alabama Bureau of Tourism and Travel, 113; Arkansas Department of Parks and Tourism, 95, 98 (both), 99 (top, bottom, center left), 100; John Bowen, 26 (top), 39, 78–79, 82, 99 (center right), 119 (inset), 126 (top and bottom left), 134, 143, 151; Georgia Tourism Division, 154, 155, 165 (bottom), 172–173; Gettysburg Tourist Council, 72 (top), 75 (both); Kansas State Historical Society, 169, 170–171, 172 (both); Kentucky Division of Tourism, 119, 138 (inset); Louisiana Office of Tourism, 107 (both); Maryland Office of Tourist Development, 67 (bottom); Mississippi Department of Economic Development, pages 146, 147, 148; Missouri Division of Tourism, 93, 94; National Archives, pages 12, 13, 17 (all), 20, 23 (top), 24 (all), 25 (both), 27 (all), 29 (both), 32, 33, 35 (inset), 40 (top), 41, 42 (top), 44, 48, 49, 50 (center right), 51 (all), 53, 57, 58 (bottom left), 62 (top left and right), 66, 68 (both), 69 (both), 71, 73 (both), 74, 77, 81 (both), 88, 105 (bottom), 108, 111, 112 (both), 120, 125, 129, 133, 135 (both), 142, 152, 156, 157, 158 (top), 159 (both), 160 (both), 161 (bottom); National Park Service, pages 10, 14 (both), 19, 23 (bottom), 24, 26 (bottom), 25 (top), 30 (bottom), 31 (both), 34–35, 43, 45, 46 (all), 47 (both), 52, 54, 67 (top), 70, 86, 87, 91 (all), 118, 122, 153, 158 (bottom), 161 (top), 162, 163 (both), 165 (top), 174, 177 (both), 178, 179 (both), 180 (both), 181; National Trust for Historic Preservation, 42 (bottom); New Mexico Tourism and Travel Division, 176; New-York Historical Society, 21, 36–37, 72 (bottom), 80, 85, 102–103, 104, 105 (top), 123 (both), 124, 125 (inset), 128, 144–145, 164; North Carolina Division of Tourism, 83; South Carolina Department of Parks, Recreation and Tourism, 15, 18; Tennessee Tourist Development Division, 126, 130, 136, 138–139; Virginia Division of Tourism, 40 (bottom), 50 (top and bottom left), 58 (top, bottom right), 49 (both), 60; West Virginia Governor's Office of Economic Development, 62 (upper right), 63, 64 (both).